Reunion

with

Death

A Meadowood Mystery

Book 2

Nancy M. Wade

Copyright

Titles of Nancy M. Wade

Circle - D Saga

Book 1 - *Endless Circle*

Book 2 - *Moment in Time*

Book 3 – *Gun for Hire (coming 2023)*

Novels:

Reflections: A Sentimental Journey

Frontier Heart

A Meadowood Mystery – Series

Scarecrows and Corpses

Reunion with Death

Deadly Bones

Berry Little Murder

Short Story

Courtship of Laura

REVIEWS

"Nancy Wade has done it again! She has created yet another delightfully suspenseful cozy mystery set in the small town of Meadowood starring the cute and curious sleuth Meredith Gardner and her faithful girl tribe. Come along as they set out to solve the mysterious death of the Class of 1996 high school reunion crasher. The stakes are upped when Meredith's own deputy husband is wrongly accused . . . or is he? You'll be guessing until the end." ~ Author, Tammy Robinson Smith

"Great mystery story. Loved all the characters and a small-town community! Good read!! "- H. Amme

Table of Contents

Chapter 1

Colleen Callahan tied a ribbon to anchor the bright yellow balloon onto the weighted base of the festive blue and gold centerpiece. The balloon floated gaily above the round banquet table, dancing lightly in the cool air conditioning. She stood back to survey the effect then moved on to the next white linen covered table with a royal blue balloon in hand and tied its ribbon to the centerpiece flower bowl.

"This is so much fun!" exclaimed Colleen as she brushed a strand of long auburn hair off a freckled cheek. Her Irish green eyes sparkled as she watched me climb atop a shaky stepladder. "Aren't you happy you volunteered?" she joked.

"Why is it, we always seem to be the only ones roped into helping? One of these days, I've got to learn how to say no. Hey, can you hold the other end of this banner until I get this side secured?" I asked Colleen, my absolute best friend since grade school.

"Oh, sure thing. Hang on. . . got it," said Colleen as she reached to grasp the paper sign proclaiming Meadowood High – 15th Class Reunion.

"Keep holding that until I get this ladder moved." I scooted the ladder to the left and climbed up the rickety steps once again. I stretched my five foot-four-inch frame then stood on tiptoes to pull the long banner into place and taped the corner to the upper doorframe. "Can you see if it's level? I'd hate to hang it crooked."

"Nope, looks great. You do good work, girl."

"Thanks. Whew, let's take a break. I could use something cold to drink," I said.

"Now that you mention it, me too."

We left the banquet room and made our way down plush carpeted hallways to the cozy coffee shop off the front lobby of the Oak Meadow Inn. Colleen approached the teenage girl behind the counter and waited while the girl finished pouring a latte that she had brewed, then served her other customer.

"Be right with you," the young gal said as she looked up.

"No problem," said Colleen as she scanned the menu posted on the back wall.

"Okay, what can I get you?"

"I just want something cold to drink. How about an unsweetened iced tea with a piece of lemon?" Colleen turned to Meredith, "Want an iced tea?" At Merry's nod, she turned back to the clerk, "Make that two."

Colleen helped herself to two long straws then carried the pair of tall icy drinks to their tiny bistro table.

"I've got this," Colleen said as she grabbed her wallet and walked back to the counter. "What do I owe you, hon?"

"Two-fifty. No tax on beverages served in-house, just take-outs."

"Thanks. Here's three, you can keep the change," Colleen told her as she paid and returned to Meredith.

Both women drank thirstily before they finally sat back in their chairs satisfied.

Colleen sighed, "I needed that. Didn't realize how dry I was."

"Mmm, totally agree. I still can't believe how lucky we were to get the Inn's banquet room for our reunion. I never would have considered Oak Meadow, way above our budget, but with the low rate Gary Bates quoted us, I just couldn't turn it down. Wait until everyone sees this place! They'll be blown away."

"What did Gary say? Why was the room available? Some kind of last-minute cancellation?" Colleen asked.

"Yeah, there was a fancy wedding booked then suddenly the groom backed out and left the bride practically standing at the altar. Poor thing. The couple had already paid a large deposit six months ago, but the Inn's policy denies any refund when they cancel without advance notice and within a few days of the event. So, Gary told me that since the Inn had collected that extra money, he just wanted to quickly rent the room again. Fortunately for us, that bride's loss is our gain," I explained.

"Well, the reunion will certainly be classy this year in this setting. Luckily for us we only had the school gymnasium booked and we could switch locations easily. You know, we may not have very many people on our committee, but I think we've done a fabulous job getting the reunion organized," Colleen said proudly.

Colleen smiled at her friend. Meredith Gardner was a gal a person could always count on to join community projects or to lend a hand when someone needed help. Her bubbly and can-do personality always saw the glass as half full. Merry might be busy with her husband Doug and two young boys plus a troop of cub scouts, but she usually managed to find time to do more when called upon.

"Hmm, did you check your emails today for any more reservations? The caterer planned a menu for sixty max. I think our last head count is up to fifty-six, that's seventy-five percent of our senior class. I kind of doubted we'd get that many people interested, didn't you?"

"I always hoped that once the invitations went out, our classmates would rally and support the idea. We had a great turnout for our tenth year. I'm more surprised that everyone's enthusiasm has already begun to diminish. What's it going to be like when we have our twenty-fifth or our fiftieth, if we live that long?" asked Colleen.

I snorted into my drink, "I don't even want to think that far into the future. Fiftieth... heaven forbid!"

"Guess we better go finish up," said Colleen as she stood then deposited her empty paper cup into a trash bin.

We strolled back to the banquet room, pinching ourselves at our good fortune to be holding the reunion in the town's, heck in the entire county's, best hotel. Oak Meadow Inn sprawled over forty-five acres of ground located just outside Meadowood's city limits.

4

Guests staying at the Inn dine at Kenyon, the four-star rated gourmet restaurant on the premises, or they can while away time on the lush, green nine-hole golf course or simply relax with a fishing rod at the nearby stream. The hotel claimed the privilege of hosting two United States Presidents and four Senators over the years since it's construction in 1948. The exterior boasted rough granite stone walls with a charcoal slate tiled roof, floor to ceiling windows, and two wide brick patios that overlooked terraces graced with fragrant gardens and artful topiary trees. A lovely gazebo located off the rear terrace provided the perfect setting for wedding ceremonies.

Inside the inn, bold timbers stretched across high cathedral ceilings in the main lobby and great room where guests can gather by a tall stone fireplace in winter or enjoy comfortable sofas and a refreshing drink in warmer seasons. Bright patterned area rugs that reflected the jewel toned fabrics of the furniture and draperies softened the hardwood floors. Framed paintings by landscape artist Debra Dawson of Denison University in Granville hung on cream-colored walls in the great room. Colorful prints of John Audubon's bird species decorated the walls of the Kenyon dining room. A peek into the Buckeye room showed scarlet and gray sports memorabilia from The Ohio State University that dated back several decades to Woody Hayes. Replicas of mascot, Brutus Buckeye, and other items hung above the bar and atop inviting bistro tables.

Warm summer sun streamed through the banquet room's sparkling clean glass window wall that overlooked the inn's gardens. It was such a pretty view; creamy white roses occupied center stage of the wide garden, bordered by rows of delicate pink and white vinca flowers. Dwarf honeysuckle bushes grew at each corner and added their fragrance to the humid air. I couldn't help but pause in our work and stare at the lush surroundings.

"Penny for your thoughts," Colleen said as she secured the last balloon.

"Oh, just admiring the view and thinking that all our hard work is paying off. When we started putting together this reunion party nine months ago, I really thought it might be a lost cause. So many people have moved away and lost touch. But now. . ."

"I know what you mean. We've had our hands full just trying to find current phone numbers and email addresses to contact all our classmates. Thank goodness for Facebook or we wouldn't have found half of these people. Do you think every class has this problem?" asked Colleen.

I stretched my arms above my head then dropped my hands to run fingers through my tousled frosted blond hair, fluffed the short curls and lifted them off the back of my neck. My shoulders and arms ached from carrying boxes and hanging decorations. I glanced about the room and began to pack up the extra streamers and balloons.

"Probably. People are so transient these days. Wasn't it nice of Gary to allow us to put up these decorations? I thought the inn would be stricter about damage to the walls and stuff, but I guess he's used to dealing with people and different kinds of party arrangements. No doubt they've hosted other reunions or birthday parties in here, not just wedding receptions. Still, I think we've been careful not to stick tape on painted walls or make nail holes." I set a box down next to the side exit door and walked back toward Colleen just as her i-phone beeped to announce an incoming message.

Colleen picked up her telephone and quickly read the text. A frown creased her brow and she raised wide eyes to me. "You're not going to believe who just texted a confirmation for the reunion."

"Okay, who? I can tell by the expression on your face you weren't expecting it. So, who?" I asked.

"Bryan Kirkland just sent his R.S.V.P. Are you going to be okay with this?" Colleen asked worriedly.

Memories and images flashed across my mind propelling me back to teenage dances and lazy afternoon picnics with Bryan holding my hand on long walks through the woods. I shook my head to banish my thoughts and raised my eyes to the concern showing in Colleen's.

"Of course, I am. Just surprised, that's all. Bryan means nothing to me now; I haven't seen him since our junior year when he quit to join the Army. We were just kids then."

"You sure it's okay? It's odd, him turning up like this and deciding to attend the reunion when he really didn't graduate with the class."

"Well, I guess he considers us his class anyway since we all went to school together practically since kindergarten. Where was that last address you sent the invitation to; someplace in California?"

"Yes, as I recall, it was Fort Irwin near Barstow. I never did know if he got it, but it didn't come back through the post office as undeliverable, so I guess he did," Colleen explained.

"Hmm... Bryan Kirkland after all these years."

"Are you going to tell Doug?" Colleen asked me as we left the party room and headed for our cars.

"I dunno. Why worry him unnecessarily?" I mused and prayed I was right.

Chapter 2

"Honey, can you help me with this zipper? I think it's stuck," I said as I twisted and turned my back toward my husband.

"Hmm, let me see this thing." His hands lightly caressed my bare shoulders before moving to the stuck zipper on my dress. I felt him tug and slide the tab downward, freeing a tiny thread of fabric, then worked it upward. "That's got it."

"What would I do without you? Thanks, honey." I slipped on a pair of white high-heeled sandals then twirled around; the soft blue chiffon skirt swirled about my knees. I adjusted the spaghetti-thin shoulder straps and ran my hand down the snug fitting bodice. "Well, what do you think?"

"I think you're gorgeous, but, ahem, do you really need to display so much cleavage tonight? I'd hate to fight off someone ogling my wife," Doug spoke in jest, but his serious eyes said otherwise.

"Douglas Gardner, I sincerely doubt anyone will have eyes on this old mother of two. But thank you for the compliment. Now that I'm in my thirties, it does make me feel good to know my husband still finds me attractive," I told him as I wrapped my arms around his broad shoulders and kissed him thoroughly.

He returned my kiss; his eyes smoldered as he conveyed a very suggestive message. "Are you sure we have to go to this thing? I can think of better ways to spend the evening."

"I'll take you up on your offer later, but yes, we have to go. I'm on the reunion committee; Colleen and I have worked our tails off to make this party special. Wait until you see how gorgeous the banquet room is at Oak Meadow. We really lucked out with this venue."

I reached for my white clutch purse as I turned on a lamp in the living room before we left. The cool sage green walls of the cozy room reflected the soft glow. Matching sage green sofa and draperies coordinated with serviceable tweed covered chairs in the room to provide a relaxed setting. French doors in the dining room glimmered with the setting sun of the early evening. As I glanced around both spaces, I couldn't help thinking how much I really admired our comfortable colonial with its large rooms and hardwood floors. It wasn't fancy, but it was home for a family of two young boys plus a furry baby. I admired the special touches that we had added over the years such as the Thomas Kinkade painting that Doug and I had splurged on for our fifth anniversary. It hung above the fireplace and was flanked by a pair of my grandmother's antique brass candlesticks on the mantle.

Mittens meowed, making his presence known and demanded to be fed before we left the house. I gave him a quick knuckle rub to the top of his head, and he purred contentedly as I placed bowls of food and fresh water on his mat.

"Behave yourself now. No chasing those birds outside," I told our orange and white tabby with one last pet.

"Rowww," Mittens replied.

Doug flicked on the outside light and locked the door behind us. I settled into the passenger seat of our worn minivan and waited for Doug to start the engine.

He grinned as he glanced my way. "Kind of feels like Friday date night again, doesn't it?"

Doug looked so handsome in his new navy-blue linen sport coat and tan dockers. He wore his white shirt unbuttoned at the neck, leaving it open and casual. My fingers toyed with fringes of his brown hair and caressed the back of his neck. *"Getting a bit shaggy back there,"* I thought to myself, *"I'll have to book him a haircut."*

I smiled warmly at this man that I loved so much and who totally completed me.

"Aren't you the romantic? It has been a very long time since we've had a chance to go anywhere without the boys. I hope Billy and Johnny are behaving themselves with your mother. Has she called today?"

Doug's parents live up in Shaker Heights, a two-hour drive away, near Lake Erie in one of the upscale neighborhoods. I know Harold and Maude Gardner love me and the kids, but his mother seems to take a particular delight in reminding Doug that he married beneath himself because I didn't finish college. I normally choose to let Doug deal with his parents, especially his mother. It helps to keep peace in the family.

"Spoke with her this morning; Mom and Dad are taking the boys over to Put-in-Bay on Bass Island. Dad plans on sailing the boat across the lake. Our boys will have a great time," said Doug.

"Lake Erie is awfully big. Do you think they'll be safe, wear life vests and everything? Your father won't take any chances, I know, but still. . ."

"They'll all be fine. Stop worrying like a mother hen and let's enjoy our time alone."

"You're right. It's just hard to stop being a mother. I'll call them in the morning," I promised, as we drove down our street and turned toward town.

Meadowood is a typical small Midwestern town. We're within driving distance to several big cities and an hour away from the Ohio state capital, but we're still basically a rural community. Rolling hills, rich with flourishing farmlands, fill the countryside that surrounds our century old town. Acres of corn or soybeans grow throughout the humid summer months, spreading across the land like a lush green quilt as they wait upon the busy autumn harvest season to arrive.

A tour of Meadowood makes you feel like you've stepped back in time with its quaint buildings and store fronts that line the main street through town. Large oak and maple trees border the streets and spread their heavy canopies of branches on each side. The usual insurance, real estate offices, and bank branches blended with various other retail businesses downtown. All were situated in brick and clapboard structures that donned gables or dormers and dated back at least a hundred years; without a single, garish neon sign to destroy the historic image. I glanced over at my Aunt Fran's dress shop,

12

Frannie's Frocks, as we drove past. I could see my aunt inside helping a late customer. I checked the time on the car's dashboard; she would be closing in a few minutes.

Doug proceeded down Park Avenue, past the intersection of Broad Street with the Sheriff's office situated on the corner then headed out of the city limits toward the inn. It was a rare event when my husband had the entire weekend off from his deputy duties; I planned to take advantage of our time together. Normally we had our eight and ten-year old sons with us but since they were spending a summer vacation week with their grandparents in Shaker Heights, we could pretend we were newlyweds again.

I smiled at Doug and he squeezed my hand as we neared the beautiful inn. Solar lights dotted both edges of the driveway that wound gracefully toward the front entrance of the stone building. Doug stopped and a valet rushed forward to open my door while another valet offered to park the car for us. Doug handed the young man his keys and a tip then offered his arm to me as we approached the lobby of Oak Meadows Inn.

My nostrils filled with the sweet fragrance of roses and honeysuckle that lined the garden pathways. Music drifted in the warm July evening; it floated on the soft breeze and beckoned us forward. As we entered, the aroma of delicious food enticed us and made my mouth water in anticipation. I hadn't realized how hungry I was until my stomach growled embarrassingly.

Doug laughed and whispered in my ear, "I don't think anyone but me heard that, but we better find some food for you."

I felt my cheeks pinken and grow warm as we headed for the banquet room and the sound of voices. My friend, Barbara Williams, greeted us as we neared the welcome table set up near the hall entrance. She looked so pretty tonight in a pale peach sheath that complimented her ginger-colored hair and fair complexion.

"Here you go," Barb said as she handed me our name tags. "Everything looks super. You and Colleen did a great job with the decorations."

"Thanks. By the way, you look lovely in that dress, Barb. Seems like we've had quite a few early arrivals. Is Colleen here?" I asked.

"Mmm-hmm, she just went to the kitchen to check on what time the servers will begin. Some folks have asked about the food and I know we had agreed the appetizers would be served first before the buffet opened but nothing has been served yet."

"I didn't think we'd have so many people arrive before seven; maybe we better ask the caterer to adjust our dining times. Honey, why don't you go in and find us some seats at table number one? Colleen and I put numbered cards in the center of each table so we can identify tables later for raffle drawings," I said.

Doug strolled into the room. He stood in the center of the floor and looked around, taking in the bright blue and gold decorations and the wide reunion banner. He located table number one then turned to greet Ron Wythe, his college football buddy and local insurance agent.

"Hey Ron, how are ya? You here with Colleen tonight?"

"Yep, I'm her plus one," Ron replied with a laugh.

"Well, buddy, it would appear we've been abandoned," Doug said with a chuckle.

"Yeah, guess duty calls."

Colleen was speaking with one of the waitresses as I entered the kitchen's outer room.

"Hi. Looks like we've got some hungry people out there; almost half of our guests have arrived early. Can I speak with Ricardo? I know he's busy, but perhaps a second of his time to ask about changing our dining schedule?" I asked the young girl as she wrung her hands and glanced nervously between Colleen and me.

She dashed off through the set of stainless-steel swinging doors into the heart of the kitchen. Sounds of pots being stirred, meat sizzling in pans, and commands quickly issued and followed drifted from the open portal. The doors had not swung shut before the head chef, Ricardo, appeared with our server hovering behind him.

"What seems to be the problem?" he inquired with a raised eyebrow and stern expression directed toward both of us.

"Um, we were wondering if the appetizers could be served now? Looks like most of our guests have arrived and I know we originally planned dinner to be ready closer to eight, but perhaps we could have something to tide folks over?" I quietly asked him.

"Maybe a fruit plate or just some cheese and crackers? Doesn't have to be anything elaborate," Colleen suggested. "I don't think the cocktail sausages and tiny spring rolls are going to be enough to hold this crowd for another hour."

Ricardo considered our request then turned to the young girl, "Joanie, you and Maria put together a tray of assorted crackers and cheese cubes plus a platter of the mixed fruit. You'll find some fruit already in a container in the walk-in refrigerator; I just prepared some for tomorrow morning's brunch. You can have that to serve." He turned to us as the girl scampered away, "Ladies, will that do? I cannot change the time of the main entrees but perhaps this will satisfy your needs?"

"Yes, that's perfect. Thank you for accommodating us. Please add the additional platters onto our bill," I replied and smiled sweetly at him.

"You'll excuse me? I've got a kitchen to run." He turned and was through the swinging doors before we could thank him again.

"Okay, that was easier than I expected," I said with a sigh of relief.

"Whew, glad you showed up when you did. Strength in numbers, and all that. I can command school children and direct teachers, but I felt at a total loss as to how to handle a disgruntled chef," Colleen admitted.

"Oh, come on! Every principal I've ever met can stand her ground and you're no different. I'm sure you would have done just fine without me," I laughed as we returned to the party and made our way through the growing crowd, back to the table and our waiting men.

"Get everything worked out?" asked Doug as he handed me a glass of white wine.

"Mmm, thanks." I placed my clutch purse on a chair seat and sipped the chilled wine. "That's good. Oak Meadow certainly has an excellent wine cellar."

"Quite the turn out," remarked Ron.

"Place looks really sharp. Nice job ladies," complimented Doug.

"Ooh, I've got to see the posters that Martha made. Come on," I said as I grabbed Doug by the hand, half dragging him, and hurried toward the opposite side of the room.

Two large styrofoam poster boards, covered in an array of photographs, perched on artist easels next to one of the tall windows that overlooked the gardens. Martha Parker stood next to the easels. She adjusted the position of the posters then stood back to admire her handiwork. Martha was normally up to her elbows in sugar and flour creating delicious treats and baked goods for her bakery in downtown Meadowood. Somehow, she had managed to steal time away from her daily chores to craft the memory boards for the reunion.

"Martha, those look great! How did you manage to track down so many photos?" I asked as I admired the high school yearbook pictures and candid shots of my fellow classmates taken fifteen or more years ago. Prom invitations, graduation programs, and sport championship memorabilia decorated one of the posters.

Colleen and Ron joined us as we crowded together in front of the posters and laughed or pointed at the pictures. Martha had captured the many special events that every class enjoys – prom night, championship basketball games, cheerleaders and football players, graduation pictures and the posed yearbook portraits.

"Where are you?" asked Doug. Douglas had gone to Worthington High School, not Meadowood, and graduated four years ahead of our class. I met him at college when he enrolled after serving in the Army. He swept me off my feet; love at first sight, and we married soon after. I finished my associate degree then quit school when I became pregnant with our son Johnny. Doug transferred to OSU to complete his bachelor's. He and Ron were both star players on the OSU football team and are still loyal Buckeyes every fall season.

I smiled at my husband and thought of all that we had missed sharing during our high school years. Still, fate had a way of intervening. Our life together now was just perfect; I wouldn't have it any other way.

"Here I am," I said as I pointed to my yearbook picture.

Doug leaned closer to study the black and white photo then scanned some of the other shots. "Was your hair that long in college? I don't think I recall you with long hair. Oh hey, is that Colleen? Even in a black and white shot, that red hair stands out."

I laughed and nodded then moved on to examine the second poster. I paused and stared at the photograph of the young couple posed in prom gown and tuxedo. My own innocent face stared right back at me. Was I ever that young?

"That's you, isn't it? Who's that with you?" asked Doug as he pointed to the picture of me wearing a crown and holding a bouquet of red roses, smiling up into the face of my date.

"Yes, I was prom queen. That's Bryan Kirkland; we dated in my junior year."

"Oh yeah? Well, I don't think I like the way he has his arm around you. Looks awfully possessive to me."

"Douglas Gardner, you can't be jealous of someone in a picture from over fifteen years ago and before I ever met you!"

"Who says I can't?" he laughed and nuzzled my neck as he pulled me closer to his side.

Naturally, as luck will have it, the class loudmouth chose that moment to push his way forward and study the picture collection, pointing and guffawing at the many faces.

"Lookee there. Merry was always in the middle of things, cheerleader or prom queen. You could count on our Meredith to be the center of attention," Herb Canter's obnoxious voice bellowed. He turned and snickered at me. "Yep, Merry and Kirkland were downright inseparable back then, quite the pair."

"Have you found your table yet, Herb? You'll need to be seated when dinner is served," I hinted not very subtly and hoped he would move on.

I felt Doug's arm stiffen and drop from around my waist as we watched the annoying man walk away and others came to view the poster collection. A frown creased his brow. I recognized the storm brewing behind those hooded eyes and sought to divert it.

"Let's get a refill of our drinks, shall we?" I suggested, slipping my arm through his and leading him toward the bar and away from those dreadful pictures. We chatted with various people, some Meadowood neighbors and others who had moved away. I delighted in introducing Doug to my old classmates as we made our way across the room.

The restaurant servers balanced silver trays of hors d'oeuvres as they moved about the mingling throng. I stopped one and selected several pieces of fruit and cheese from the platter and placed the snacks on a small plate. My stomach growled again in anticipation as I popped a strawberry into my mouth.

People stood about nibbling on the food, greeting past friends and chatting amiably. Donna Simon waved a hello as she and her husband Tom grabbed some cheese and crackers. We are such a small community, I know so many people here tonight; some because we're past classmates and others because I lead their children within my Cub Scout den, or I include the women among my Avon customers. Donna fits into all three categories. Doug and I approached a group by the bar then selected a fresh glass of wine for me and another beer for himself.

"Oh, hey Pete, I wanted to ask you to say a few words to the class before the buffet dinner is called," I said as I greeted my friend Carol and her husband Pete Goodwin, our senior class president.

"Uh, I guess I can. Kind of unexpected, Merry. Geez, you could give a fella more notice. What do you want me to say?" Pete murmured.

20

"Sorry, Pete. You're right; I should have asked you before this. Just welcome everyone as the class president and announce that dinner will be served, and that the reunion committee will be selling 50-50 raffle tickets throughout the night. That's all. Short and sweet. I'll be there with you."

"Yeah, okay. I guess I can do that. Let me know when," Pete reluctantly agreed. He reached for another beer before he and Carol strolled back toward their table.

Chapter 3

I slid into my seat, juggling the snack plate while setting my wine glass down. It felt good to sit down and get off my feet; I wasn't used to walking around in high heels. I breathed a sigh of relief.

"My feet are killing me. How do you do it?" I asked Colleen as she smiled at me sympathetically. I noticed she wore strappy four-inch stiletto heels that perfectly matched her emerald, green satin cocktail dress.

"Guess I'm used to it. I'm in heels and business attire every day. Believe me, I look forward to weekends and tennis shoes."

I nodded then glanced about the room. Most of our classmates had remained in Ohio, not all stayed local in Meadowood, but at least most had stayed within the state. We did have a few adventuresome folks that had ventured to other lands for school and careers.

"Isn't that Joe Spellman standing over by the doorway? I heard he lives in Florida now and works as an oceanographer. Can you imagine? He was so shy in high school; I never got to know him very well," I said.

"I had a chance to speak to him for a moment. He's come with his wife Maddie and they have six children. Guess he got over his shyness," Colleen said with a giggle.

"No! Really? Holy cow."

"By the way, did you speak to Pete?" asked Colleen.

"Yes. He'll do it. I guess I shouldn't have broadsided him like that and should have given him more of a head's up. But he'll be fine; he's used to speaking to groups. Just look at all the tours he does for the fire station as the chief's spokesperson and when he does his talks about fire safety at school for the children. He's a great public speaker."

Colleen glanced at Ron and Doug deep in football talk before leaning close to whisper to me, "Have you seen, you know who?"

"Is he here yet?"

"Barb told me she's checked in everyone and all the name tags are gone from the welcome table, so I assume he's in the room somewhere," said Colleen as she scanned the crowd.

I tried to glance about the room, surreptitiously studying faces to try and recognize Bryan when my line of vision was blocked suddenly by the waitress standing by my chair.

"Mrs. Gardner, we're ready for the buffet now. Would you make the announcement to your group, please?"

"Um, sure. Thanks," I mumbled as I got to my feet again and went in search of Pete Goodwin. I found him quickly then led him to the center of the floor where we stood for a moment trying to decide how best to get everyone's attention. I tried clapping my hands loudly when suddenly a commanding voice shouted from behind me.

"Ladies and gentlemen, may we have your attention please!"

I turned to thank the announcer and stared into the face of Bryan Kirkland. A myriad of emotions flashed across my face before I gained my composure and faced the expectant crowd.

"If everyone will find your dining table and take a seat, our buffet dinner will begin soon. But first, we'll hear from our class president, Pete Goodwin." I moved aside for Pete and when I turned, Bryan had melted into the crowd.

Pete cleared his throat then spoke in a loud voice, "Welcome everyone to the fifteenth reunion of the Meadowood High School Class of 1996. Thank you all for coming. Let's give a round of applause to our reunion committee for organizing this great party and weekend activities."

Exuberant applause filled the room along with a few whistles of appreciation. I raised my hands to quiet the crowd before continuing my announcement.

"Thank you everyone. Before we enjoy our delicious dinner, I want to remind you that we'll be meeting for a fun day of picnics and volleyball games at the Fox Run Park starting tomorrow morning at eleven o'clock. Also, committee members are selling 50/50 raffle tickets; be sure and buy several for a chance at the jack pot."

The waitress Joanie stepped forward and waited on my nod to continue with her own announcement, "We will call you to the buffet by table numbers, two at a time, starting with table numbers one and two. You can begin now. Please line up on both sides of the buffet."

A murmur of approval ran through the room as I joined Doug waiting in line with Colleen, Ron, Ted and Barb Williams from our table. Table two occupants lined up on the opposite side of the buffet line. I reached for the spoon handle inside a bowl of broccoli salad when a hand casually captured mine. I raised my eyes from the tempting assortment of food to see Bryan Kirkland standing before me once again. I stood transfixed.

"Hello again," he said in a suave voice while his eyes rudely slid up and down my body. "You look fantastic, Merry, especially in that dress. You haven't changed in all these years, except maybe your short hair. I like it."

"Harrumph," Doug grunted, reminding me of his presence and bringing my attention back to him.

"Um, Bryan Kirkland, I'd like to introduce my husband, Douglas Gardner," I stammered. I cast a quick glance at my husband, "Doug, this is Bryan ..."

"I know who he is," Doug interrupted me, scowled at Bryan and tossed me a look of annoyance as my answer.

"Hey, you guys, let's get this line moving," Ron joked as he took in the scene and tried to relieve the thick tension. "Food smells delicious."

I held my plate and moved ahead toward the hot entrees, deciding to concentrate on the food and not what had just happened. Ron was right, the display of menu items did indeed smell and appear enticing. A large platter of spicy, Stroganoff meatballs accompanied a bowl of steaming, buttered egg noodles. A chafing dish contained boiled red potatoes, and sauteed green beans. Wedges of grilled salmon rested atop a layer of rice pilaf. Tender roasted chicken breasts completed the hot entrees offered along with bowls of broccoli salad or a tossed garden salad for the more diet conscious diner.

I selected the salmon and rice, added a warm dinner roll and decided to treat myself to the dessert table too. Ricardo's dessert choices were perfect for a warm summer night – angel food cake with a sweet strawberry sauce, a platter filled with various cookies, and icy, orange sorbet parfaits. I opted for the angel food cake with a spoonful of strawberries on top.

We managed to return to our table before the others. As Doug placed his plate of chicken, potatoes and green beans onto the table, he turned to me with an inquiring expression on his face.

"You want to tell me what that was all about? Thought that dude was in your past?" he snapped.

"He is. It just surprised me being confronted by him like that. I don't have any feelings for him. Please don't make a big fuss over nothing," I pleaded in a loud whisper that began to draw attention.

Colleen and Ron shot questioning glances at us as they pretended to be preoccupied with their plates. I lowered my head and played with my own food, jabbing a fork into the flaky salmon. I abruptly pushed my chair back and stood up.

"I need some air," I declared and walked hurriedly from the room, trying not to make a scene as my anger built over my husband's unwarranted attitude. I didn't ask for Bryan's attention, Doug should realize that. I admitted to myself that Bryan's actions made me feel uncomfortable and I wasn't sure why.

I hurried into the ladies' room located off the short side hallway near the garden exit, then stood staring at my image reflected in the mirror as I tried to calm down and sort out my own emotions. Did I still have feelings for Bryan? No, of course not. He's part of my past and it's only seeing him again in this damn reunion that dredges up old memories and teenage crushes. A noise in one of the stalls interrupted my introspection. I hurriedly squirted soap onto my hands and held them under the running water. I glanced up at the woman stepping toward the sink.

"Hello," I greeted automatically as I glanced at her and noticed her manner of dress. Her cotton sundress was clean and cute but too young of a style for a woman clearly in her thirties. The rubber flip-flop sandals on her feet definitely appeared inappropriate for a formal party. I met her eyes in the mirror as I inquired, "Having a good time at the party? Are you a guest? With someone?"

"Uh, ahem," she started then swallowed, "I'm not at the party, just looking for a friend who's supposed to be here."

"Oh, maybe I can help you find him or her. What's the name?"

"Thanks, but that's all right. I'm leaving," she said and quickly left the restroom.

I stood staring at the closed door. *"Humph, not my problem. Guess I better get back,"* I thought to myself as I dried my hands and left the bathroom.

Angry voices outside drew my attention to the exit door nearby. The door stood ajar; I opened it further and stepped out into the fragrant garden patio. I blinked as I waited for my eyes to adjust to the darkness. Dim light radiated from round solar lights among the plants and illuminated the stone walkway but little else. I had taken a few stealthy steps forward when I heard the distinct crack of a hand slapping a cheek. I stood listening, straining to hear more.

"What are you doing here?" a deep voice snarled. The voice sounded vaguely familiar.

"I want my money," a woman demanded.

I moved toward the corner of the building. I could only make out the shape of a woman gesturing wildly to someone standing deep in the shadows. He growled something to her, but the sudden volume of noise and music that flowed from the open side entry swallowed his words. I turned around and saw Colleen standing next to the door.

"Looking for me?" I asked as I stepped back into the circle of bright light above the doorway.

"Yes. Doug is brooding. I told him you were probably just in the restroom, but I thought I'd better find you."

"Well, I was, so you weren't lying. I just stepped outside for some air." I pointed to the dark corner, "I think I heard someone arguing back there."

"I don't hear anything. Maybe they left," Colleen suggested.

"Yeah, maybe. Let's get back inside before my husband puts out an all-points bulletin on me. Did he appear really mad? I can't get over how jealous he got, even though Bryan's behavior toward me was rude and way too familiar. Bryan never used to be that way."

"I'm sorry. I should never have invited Bryan," Colleen said as we walked past groups of people milling about the buffet table and bar.

"It's not your fault." We returned to an empty table with only Ted Williams still seated.

"Where's Doug?" I asked Ted.

"Don't know. He disappeared shortly after you left."

"Oh my," I mumbled, unsure of how to mend my marital harmony.

Before I had time to worry about my husband's absence, Martha and Barb approached me with the container of raffle tickets.

"We sold all our tickets. Isn't that marvelous?" exclaimed Martha.

"Before it gets too late, we want to draw the winning raffle ticket," stated Barb.

"Okay, good idea. Ask for a volunteer to pull a ticket and have Pete announce the winner," I instructed then turned back to our empty table.

Someone had cleared away my plate of cold food. I didn't realize how long I'd been gone. At least my dessert was still there, and I dropped onto my chair intending to put something into my empty stomach. *God, I wish I had a cup of coffee.* My prayers were suddenly answered when a cup of steaming hot coffee plus a fresh plate of food miraculously appeared in front of me.

A warm hand rested on my bare shoulder as my husband bent to whisper in my ear, "Forgive me? I was acting like an ass."

29

"Yes. Thank you for the food. I'm starving. And... I'm sorry too."

Doug kissed me lightly then slid into his own seat. He took a large sip of a fresh beer and sat back in his chair; his good humor restored. I gulped my food down as the music started playing and couples moved onto the center dance floor.

Colleen and Ron laughed as they expertly danced the latest steps. I smiled at my friends, such a perfect couple; she with her Irish coloring and slender figure and he with his bulky frame and dark Celtic features. Ron Wythe has been courting Colleen for the past two years, but she just keeps him at arm's length. Honestly, I don't know why she can't commit to the man; he's obviously bonkers over her. I admit I've tried playing Cupid occasionally, always arranging some event to throw them together. Ron's a catch, handsome and prosperous, and my dear friend Colleen deserves the best.

The dance floor filled with couples, reliving memories of sock hops or homecoming balls and other high school socials. Doug and I watched for awhile, until the music changed to a slow number.

"Shall we?" I asked Doug as I placed my hand on his arm and nodded toward the dance floor.

"Absolutely, Mrs. Gardner."

My husband took me into his arms; we listened to the band play one of our favorite romantic songs as we glided together in the slow dance. I reveled in the intimate moment until a hand abruptly tapped Doug on his shoulder and we stopped to stare at Bryan Kirkland's leering face.

"May I cut in? For old time's sake."

"No. Stay the hell away from my wife, Kirkland, or you'll be sorry," Doug ordered then turned his back on Bryan.

Bryan reached to capture my arm, but I took a step backwards. He stumbled as his feet twisted then caught himself.

"What are you going to do about it, huh? Mister tough guy. You don't look so tough," Kirkland slurred loudly.

"You're drunk, Kirkland."

Doug raised one arm to ward off Bryan's second lunge for me, resulting in Bryan only clutching empty air. We left him standing alone, swaying slightly, in the middle of the floor.

The crowd had suddenly hushed as everyone stared at the erupting scene. Doug quickly steered me toward the opposite side of the room and out the open garden doors. We stepped into the fragrant night and sought a spot away from prying eyes.

"What's gotten into you?" I hissed. I searched his face in the dim light, looking for an explanation.

"Me? What about Kirkland? Hey, I'm sorry. It's that jerk; something about him. I can't put my finger on it, but he rubs me the wrong way. The thought of him putting his hands on you, even for a simple dance. . . I, well, it made me see red."

Doug ran his hands through his hair and paced back and forth before he turned to me then gathered me in his arms in a crushing embrace. We stood clinging to each other; I could feel and hear the pounding of our hearts.

"You've got nothing to be worried about; he was in my life a very long time ago. He's nothing. Forget him, please," I pleaded. I stroked his cheek with my palm then drew his lips to mine to seal my promise with a searing kiss.

I pressed my head against his shoulder and stood within the circle of his arms. Time stood still for us as we held each other for what seemed like hours, but in reality, must have been only minutes.

"Ahem, sorry to interrupt. You guys okay?" Colleen asked in a hushed voice.

"We're fine. Just needed a moment alone, that's all," I replied as Doug and I broke apart and faced our friend.

"Party's breaking up. Gary told me we can clean up in the morning as long as we're done by ten o'clock," Colleen said.

"Great. We can take down the decorations before we go to the park. I'm not exactly in the mood to tackle that tonight," I admitted.

"No, I didn't think you would be. We're all tired. It can wait until tomorrow. I've got to go find Ron to drive me home."

"Fine. I'll see you in the morning. And Colleen. . . thanks."

The next day would prove to be a long one and the most frightening one in my life.

Chapter 4

I awoke to the smell of bacon cooking. My stomach rumbled in anticipation as I hopped out of bed and dashed into the bathroom to complete my morning ablutions. I dressed hurriedly in blue capris and a striped blue and white tank top then tucked my feet into a pair of Sketchers and dashed downstairs. I hate arguing with my husband and hope we never do again. However, making up could be very satisfying, I thought to myself with a smile on my face as I bounced into the kitchen. I wrapped my arms around Doug's waist and hugged his back as he stood at the stove scrambling eggs for our breakfast.

"Sleep well?" he asked with a knowing grin.

"Absolutely! Mmm, and he even cooks," I said with a laugh. "Good morning to you too, Mittens. Has daddy fed you yet?"

"Rwoww," Mittens replied as he rubbed against my legs.

I took that for a "no", so I picked up his bowl, gave it a quick scrub and filled it with his favorite cat nibbles. Some fresh water and a small dish of milk should hold him for the day. He meowed his approval and lapped the milk in appreciation.

Doug filled our plates and we both hopped up onto bar stools to enjoy a relaxed breakfast at the speckled granite kitchen counter.

"Mmm, I think you fix eggs better than I do," I said between bites. "You'll have to tell me your secret."

"Ah, a gourmet chef never tells," Doug said as he kissed my cheek and leaned closer to steal one of my bacon slices.

33

"Hey, you. That's not fair," I said with a jab to his ribs. "We need to get going and I still have to pack our picnic basket."

"Let's just stop at KFC along the way to the park; take that to the picnic, no fuss and no muss. With any luck, we won't have to share either," he chuckled.

When we arrived at Oak Meadow Inn, Colleen and Ron were already busy clearing tabletops, deflating balloons, and placing trash into large black bags.

"Morning! See you two got an early start," I greeted as we entered the banquet room. "Doug, can you find the step ladder? I left it in a hall closet."

"Everything okay with you?" asked Colleen with a nod in Doug's direction.

"Mmm-hm, better than okay," I answered with a broad grin.

"Good, I'm glad. Let's make short work of this. No doubt the clean-up will go lots quicker than the time it took us to put it all up."

I glanced about the room, surveying what still needed to be done, then pulled down some streamers and filled a trash bag. I picked up the two posters and carried them back to Colleen.

"I think Martha should keep these since she did so much work on them, don't you? She spent alot of time finding all these pictures," I said.

"I agree. Hey, that's funny. Look. There's an empty space on this poster," Colleen said.

I studied the grouping and realized what had occupied the empty spot. "My prom picture with Bryan had been pinned there."

"That's odd; who would have taken that picture?"

"Maybe it just fell off the board?" I speculated. We laid the poster aside and continued with our work.

Doug stood on the ladder and tugged on the banner while Ron caught it as it fell to the floor. The guys easily folded it like a twin-size bed sheet then placed it on the table by me and Colleen.

"What do you plan on doing with this?" asked Doug.

"I dunno, maybe we should take it to the park and hang it on the picnic shelter to designate our reserved tables," I suggested. "What do you think Colleen. Can we reuse it?"

"I suppose so. Is that everything?" she asked as she glanced about the empty room. "Gary said his staff will take care of the linens and the tables. Do you want one of these centerpieces to take home? Flowers are still fresh," said Colleen.

"You take one and I'll take one. I hate throwing them away; let's see if we can combine some of the flowers, stuff them into one of these vases," I said as I plucked carnations from a centerpiece and added it to the vase in front of me. "We can discard some of the greenery, it's just filler anyway." In a few minutes, we were satisfied with two full vases.

Ron carried both vases and tucked the folded banner under his arm and headed to the parking lot. Doug hefted two trash bags while Colleen and I followed him with two others out the side entrance.

"I think there's a dumpster behind here, maybe around the corner," I said. We followed the pavement to the rear of the building and saw the dumpster in question.

Suddenly, Colleen screamed. I stifled my own shriek, caught like a lump in my throat as I stopped, frozen, and stared at bloody legs protruding from the top of the dumpster. One foot still wore a rubber flip-flop sandal, the other was bare.

"Oh my God," I whispered. Trash bags dropped and forgotten, Colleen and I clasped hands, offering each other comfort.

"Stay there," ordered Doug as he stepped forward and peered into the dumpster; he turned and looked at me then shook his head side to side. It wasn't good.

Doug quickly grabbed his cell phone from his pocket and punched in 9-1-1 to call for help. I listened to him identify himself and our location as my numb mind kept seeing the woman from the restroom, wearing a cotton dress and flip-flops. Was this her body?

Ron walked around the side of the building from the parking lot looking for us, then stopped in his tracks when he saw us huddled together. His eyes grew wide with shock as he spotted the dumpster.

"Holy sh... what happened?" Ron exclaimed in disbelief.

Sirens wailed from a distance as emergency vehicles approached the Oak Meadows Inn. By now a crowd of people had formed outside, the Inn manager and several staff members including cooks and kitchen help. Everyone stepped back and allowed space for the arriving vehicles. Someone thought to turn off the siren, but multiple red lights still flashed on the vehicles, creating a strange strobe effect.

36

I watched hypnotized, unable to move or shift my eyes from the grizzly sight.

Tony Dalton, the young rookie deputy at the station, climbed out of his police cruiser and rushed toward Doug and me. Doug stepped forward to speak with the deputy.

"Hey Tony. Where's Simmons?" asked Doug as he watched two Ohio State troopers join the scene.

"Chief got called out of town; family emergency or something. We're really short-handed," Tony explained.

"What's with the troopers?"

"Uh, um, I called them. Geez, a murder like this... I mean, I can't handle this. So, I uh, thought I better," stammered Dalton nervously.

"Who said anything about a murder? You shouldn't jump the gun like that Tony and make assumptions when you get a call about a dead body, it could have been an accident or even a suicide. Just don't go off half-cocked, okay? Did you really have to call in the state guys? We could have handled this in house. I would have come back off of leave," Doug stated as he and Tony stood to one side while the state troopers took charge.

The troopers slowly canvassed the perimeter, noted the trash bags on the ground, the proximity of the dumpster to the building, and the position of the body. The older of the two men appeared to be in charge as he barked orders to his subordinate then turned to survey the crowd. A stenciled name badge affixed to his uniform identified him as Blackburn.

"I want photographs of all of this," he told his partner, Trooper Dickinson. Then he faced the crowd of onlookers, "Who found the body?" he inquired in a commanding tone.

"We did," Doug answered as he stepped forward. "I'm deputy Douglas Gardner with the Meadowood sheriff's department and this is my wife Meredith. We found the body about twenty minutes ago when we were dumping those trash bags."

"Touch anything?" questioned the state police officer.

"No, sir. I called 9-1-1 as soon as we saw the body."

"You're a deputy? And I suppose you just happened to be on the scene. Rather convenient," scoffed Sgt. Blackburn.

Doug bristled at the man's attitude but kept his cool and remained professional as he tried to explain. "I attended a party here last night. My wife, her friends and I offered to help clean up this morning. That's why we were here. We just finished collecting decorations and crap from the banquet room, bagged it up, and were about to toss them into the dumpster when we spotted the, um, legs."

"Uh huh. What kind of party?"

I stepped forward, my voice shook as I answered, "A class reunion. My high school class reunion."

"All right, boys, get her out of there. Let's see what we've got," the officer directed the pair of paramedics and trooper Dickinson. "Where's the coroner? He should be here by now."

One of the paramedics spoke up, "Uh, the Knox County coroner is in Mt. Vernon; Doc Stone is filling in for him this weekend. We called him, he's on his way now."

"You," he pointed to Tony, "clear this area. Move these people back and get everyone's name. I'll want to speak to all of them."

Tony nodded his affirmation and walked toward the group of gawking people. He withdrew a notepad from his pocket and started jotting down names and phone numbers plus their positions at Oak Meadow Inn. I saw Ricardo glance toward the dumpster and shake his head negatively as he spoke to the young deputy. Gary Bates stood to the side with arms crossed and solemnly watched the proceedings.

The two state troopers examined the now empty dumpster and quietly conferred together. The younger man leaned into the dumpster as he searched for evidence; his body hung half in and out of the steel container, oddly resembling the position of the dead woman they had just removed.

"Don't see anything else, boss. No purse, no missing shoe," stated Dickinson. "Not much blood in there either."

A battered Ford Explorer slowly drove across the paved lot and pulled onto the grassy area before coming to a stop near us. Doctor Tom Stone climbed out of the SUV, picked up his black medical bag from the front seat, slipped on a pair of rubber gloves, and strolled toward us. He obviously was in no hurry; besides, it wasn't in his nature to rush about frantically. Tom Stone hailed from Alabama but had gone to medical school at OSU close to thirty years ago then decided to stay and build his medical practice in the rural Ohio regions. His gentle southern manners and soft-spoken speech reassured and comforted his patients.

The doctor knelt down next to the body lying on the stretcher. His hands carefully explored the bloody garments, examined the body's level of lividity and temperature. He noted the signs of purple bruising on upper arms and the ashen skin color. He gently closed the wide eyes that permanently registered her surprise or fear, then the doctor stood and faced the state policeman.

"Where did you find the young lady?" asked the doctor.

"They stuffed her in that dumpster, doc. Cause of death?" replied Blackburn.

"How long do you figure she's been dead?" Dickinson interjected.

"I'll need to do a full post-mortem, but I'd speculate cause of death was multiple stab wounds to the abdomen by a long slim knife, at least ten hours ago. Who is she?"

"Good question," said Blackburn. "Does anyone know the identity of this woman?" he inquired of the group of people still assembled.

My legs shook and I whispered in a trembling voice as I stared at the woman's lifeless body on the stretcher. "I saw her here last night."

"What's her name?" demanded Blackburn.

"I . . . don't know. I met her in the bathroom. I, uh, asked her if she was with someone at the party – she said no. Then she left. I

40

think I remember she mentioned that she was looking for someone. That's all I know," I croaked. I suddenly felt chilled and began to shake.

Doug wrapped his arms around me, infusing warmth into my body. "She's in shock," Doug said. I heard his voice from far away as I floated down a dark tunnel and fainted.

Doug watched a paramedic immediately wrap a blanket around Meredith as Doctor Stone pressed two fingers against her wrist and checked her pulse. "Let's get her inside," the doctor drawled as Doug carried his wife into the cooler banquet hall.

Doctor Stone whispered to Gary Bates, the inn manager, "Got a shot of bourbon handy?"

"Sure thing, Doc," Gary replied as he hurried to the serving bar inside the party room. A minute later he returned with a shot glass and a bottle of Jim Beam.

The doctor poured a small dram of the amber liquid into the glass then held it to Meredith's lips.

A few drops of whiskey seared a path down my throat. I coughed and spluttered as my eyes flew open and I stared into the concerned face of my husband and the twinkling eyes of Tom Stone.

"Thought that would do it," the doctor laughed. "No sense wasting the rest of this fine bourbon," he said as he tossed back the remaining shot of liquor. "Ahh, that's fine whiskey." He closed his eyes for a moment in appreciation.

"She okay, Doc?" asked Doug.

"She'll be fine. Just take her home and take it easy the rest of the day. Standing out there in this heat and seeing that poor woman; too much of a shock."

"I'm right here, you know. You're both talking about me as if I'm in another room. What about the reunion picnic at the park? We're supposed to be there. Everyone will wonder what happened to us?" I stated.

Ron and Colleen had taken refuge in the banquet hall during the past half hour while the gruesome investigation had progressed. Colleen's face showed she was still shaken but Ron got up and joined Doug as he glanced at Meredith and then back at Colleen.

"It's past twelve o'clock; how about you take the girls home and I'll head over to the park to inform everyone they're on their own. Some folks will probably just picnic and call it an early day, maybe some others will still want to get a volleyball team together. It doesn't really matter, does it?" suggested Ron.

"Thanks Ron. I'll drop Colleen off at her home. I think both girls have had enough excitement for one day," Doug agreed.

A commotion outside drew our attention and within seconds, Tony and Officer Dickinson marched into the hall. Tony looked nervous and guilty while Dickinson appeared determined.

"What's going on?" Doug questioned as he met the lawmen.

"Doug, I think you better step outside," a grim Tony Dalton directed.

Chapter 5

Medical personnel had loaded the body into the ambulance by the time Doug and I stepped outside. I had insisted on staying with Doug. I gripped his hand as we faced trooper Blackburn.

"What's going on?" Doug asked again as he glanced between his fellow deputy and the state police officer.

"We just got a report of another stabbing victim over at the hospital. Some fella, Kirkland, stumbled in late last night with a knife wound to his shoulder, non-life threatening."

"So? What's that got to do with me?" asked Doug.

At that moment, I noticed Herb Canter standing among the crowd of onlookers. What was he doing here? Herb crept forward when Blackburn signaled him.

"Sir, what was your name again? Can you repeat what you told the other officer?" Blackburn inquired.

"Um, uh, my name is Herb Canter. I was here last night when, um, Doug here, threatened some woman then got into a fight with a dude from our reunion."

"Whaaat? I did no such thing," shouted Doug. "Just who was this woman I'm supposed to have threatened?"

"I dunno. She wasn't part of our class, but I heard her scream."

"He's lying!" I cried as I clung to Doug's arm, my eyes searched the faces of the men circled around us.

"I'm telling the truth," Herb insisted. "You heard it too, Meredith. I stepped out for a smoke and I saw you back here; you must've heard the woman. She was scared, you could hear it in her voice."

"Did you see this man arguing with the woman?" Blackburn questioned as he pointed to Doug.

"Well, not exactly, but I heard his voice. I'm pretty sure it was him. He had just stormed out of the party, then I saw him and Bryan Kirkland start a fight right over there," Herb accused as he pointed to a place outside the kitchen door. "They were both stinking drunk. I don't touch liquor, myself, but . . ."

"You're sure of this?" asked Dickinson as he filled his notebook.

"Yeah, sure. It was really dark back here last night but I knew who it was 'cause they almost threw punches at each other again later on the dance floor. Like two big dogs fighting over a bitch, sorry Merry. They really hate each other," Herb snickered.

I yearned to wipe the smug expression off Herb's face as he stood making his false accusations.

"This true?" Blackburn asked as he faced Doug again.

"It's true that Bryan Kirkland and I exchanged some words; I didn't like his attentions toward my wife. We spoke for a few minutes outside, but that's all. There wasn't any fight. I went back inside. I swear, I never saw any woman and I sure as hell did not knife anyone," Doug stated.

Blackburn turned to me and I felt my mouth go dry in anticipation of his next question.

"Want to tell me what really happened, Mrs. Gardner?"

"Oh dear. Bryan Kirkland and I dated in high school, that's all. I haven't seen him for over fifteen years. He made a pest of himself last night; I think he had too much to drink. I walked outside for some air, back here near the gardens."

"What time was this? Did you hear anything?"

"Shortly after dinner was served, so maybe close to eight-thirty. I think I heard some voices arguing over there, but it was too dark to see anyone and what with all the noise from the party, I didn't hear much."

"What did you hear?" the trooper questioned. He studied my face as I glanced at Doug and then back to the officer.

"Um, I may have heard a woman say something like she wanted her money. She sounded furious. Then I think a man answered her, I can't be sure. They were farther away from me and I didn't stay; my friend Colleen found me then we went back inside to the party."

"Is that all?"

"Officer Blackburn, if it had been my husband arguing with that young woman, I'm sure I would have recognized his voice. I tell you it was not him."

Blackburn turned his attention to Doug again. "What were you and Kirkland fighting about? Was it another woman? Maybe you didn't like him horning in on your wife and your mistress?"

"You're crazy!" Doug exclaimed.

"Dickinson," ordered Blackburn, "put the cuffs on this man. He's coming with us for more questioning and until we get a statement from the injured man at the hospital."

"Am I being arrested?" Doug demanded.

"Let's just say we want to talk with you further as a person of interest."

I wrapped my arms around my husband, clinging to him until the officer twisted his arms behind him and attached the pair of handcuffs. Tears ran down my face unheeded; I felt so powerless knowing my husband could not have committed this horrible crime. But how could I prove it?

"Call our lawyer," Doug called out to me as they lowered him into the back seat of the police cruiser.

I quivered in fear as I watched them drive away. Ron and Colleen gathered me in a group hug. Our class reunion had turned into a nightmare.

Chapter 6

Colleen and I slowly drove home; both of us silent, lost in our own thoughts. Ron had decided to go over to the park and update the reunion crowd on the day's events. I glanced at Colleen as I stopped my minivan in front of her house.

"Will you be okay?" we both asked simultaneously, then laughed and suddenly the tension broke.

I leaned over from behind the wheel and we hugged fiercely. A tear crept down my cheek and I wiped it away as I tried to put on a brave face.

"What are you going to do now?" asked Colleen.

I took a deep breath and exhaled before I answered her. "I don't know. I've got to do something. Call our lawyer, I suppose. Then I guess, I should call my in-laws and ask them to keep the boys."

"Will you tell them that Doug's in jail?"

"Oh my gosh, no. No sense in worrying them; he isn't formally charged and once the facts come out, I know he'll be released. This is just so unbelievable. And that Herb Canter. . . why would he say those things about Doug? The little creep. He was always harassing me in high school. He doesn't even know my husband. And what about Bryan? Do you think he accused Doug of stabbing him?"

"Maybe we should go talk to him? Do you think he's still in the hospital? What was it that state police officer said - Bryan had a knife

47

wound? Would the hospital release him by now?" Colleen speculated, glancing at her watch.

"Let's do it now," I decided suddenly. "You game?"

"Okay, let's go. I feel partially responsible for inviting him to the reunion in the first place," Colleen replied as she shut the car door and reached for her seat belt.

I jammed the gear shift lever into drive, and we sped away; headed for the county hospital and a confrontation. Within minutes I had traveled down Park and onto State Route 20 where the county hospital and medical center buildings occupied acres of ground outside Meadowood city limits and halfway between our town and Rockport, a neighboring community. I pulled into the visitor parking lot at the hospital then Colleen and I made our way into the lobby to seek the patient information desk.

"Hi, I'd like to check on the status of a patient, please," I said.

"Patient's name? Are you a relative?" asked the receptionist.

"Patient is Bryan Kirkland, and no, I'm just a friend."

The gal's fingers flew over a computer keyboard, typed in the name and clicked on her mouse. "Hmm, let's see. Mister Kirkland is in satisfactory condition. I can't give you any more details than that."

"I understand. Is he allowed visitors? Perhaps I can just pop in to say hello."

"Fourth floor, room 2-B. Visiting hours end at three o'clock," the aide informed us.

"Thank you. We won't stay long," I promised as we hurried to the elevators.

Colleen stood tapping her foot and I clasped and unclasped my hands as we watched the numbers blink and change above the elevator panel until doors finally slid open on our floor. We had to step aside to allow several people to disembark then scooted into the elevator before the doors closed. I gave the panel a quick glance and punched the number four for Bryan's floor.

"I have no idea what I am going to say to him," I whispered to Colleen.

Soft instrumental music played from a speaker over my head. A candy striper stood in the corner behind us; she studied the lit floor numbers as the elevator rose and stopped at each floor.

"Excuse me," the young girl spoke softly as she moved forward and exited onto the third floor.

"Here we go," Colleen said as the doors slid closed and the elevator rose upward, arriving on the fourth floor.

We tentatively stepped out and studied the room number signs posted on the wall before us. Rooms one through ten were located on the right while rooms eleven through twenty went toward the left hallway. We turned right and walked toward the open doorway of room 2-B.

I rapped lightly on the door then stepped into the space. Bryan sat on the side of his bed wearing a pair of black pants and had bent forward to pull on a pair of socks. His chest was bare except for the large gauze bandage that wrapped around it and across the right shoulder. A sling held his right arm secure. He looked up as we approached. I caught his rapid look of surprise before he carefully arranged his features.

"Hi Bryan. How are you?" I stammered nervously. Now that I was here, I wasn't at all sure this was a good idea.

"Merry! Well, I must say you're the last person I expected to show up here."

"I, ah, just wanted to see, um, that is, I need to ask you a question. Did you tell the police that my husband stabbed you?" I blurted out then studied his eyes and tried to read what was going on in his mind. Would he admit he falsely accused Doug?

"So that's what this brief visit is about. And here I thought you were worried and cared about my well-being," Bryan snorted with a sound that ended in a cough. "It only hurts when I laugh."

Colleen waited near the doorway. I could see her slight nod of encouragement. She tried to nonchalantly study the furnishings of the hospital room. A privacy curtain divided the center of the room and was drawn closed around the other bed and occupant.

"What happened, Bryan? How did you get hurt?" I asked with no pretext of concern now. His attitude irritated me; I began to understand what Doug had meant.

"Obviously, I got stabbed. You really should keep that husband of yours under control. He's got a wicked temper," Bryan sneered.

"Are you telling me that Doug did this? I don't believe you. What did you tell the police?" I demanded.

"I told them the truth; we had an argument last night and he coaxed me outside then attacked me." Bryan reached for his shirt tossed onto the foot of the bed. It contained blood stains across the shoulder and a short tear. He slid his left arm into one sleeve and attempted to pull the shirt across his bandaged shoulder.

I watched his futile efforts then stepped forward and gave him some assistance with the shirt, although his actions and attitude didn't deserve any acts of kindness. I yanked the wrinkled and soiled shirt across his shoulder and over the sling then buttoned a few bottom buttons to hold it closed and in place. I stared at his chest and bare shoulder; fond memories of frolicking on the beach and summer swim parties popped into my mind. I shook my head to ban those thoughts then diverted my eyes from the tan skin. Some tiny memory tickled the back of my mind and I couldn't quite put my finger on it. I took a deep breath and stepped back.

"Where's that nurse?" Bryan demanded. "I want out of here; I've got things to do."

"Bryan, I ask you again – how did you get wounded? Who really did this to you? I know my husband is innocent."

"I said all I'm going to. Maybe you don't know him as well as you think," he said as he stood up and slid his feet into his shoes.

"If you had any feelings for me in the past, I beg you to recant," I pleaded. I touched his arm, but he pulled away and pressed the nurse call button.

"Let's go," Colleen said as she pushed me into the hall.

As soon as I got home, I grabbed my personal address book then quickly flipped through the pages until I located the listing and phone number for Attorney Walter Reagan. I punched in the numbers and waited impatiently while it rang. Finally, after the fifth ring, a breathless voice answered.

"Hello, office of Reagan and Wilson. This is Jody; how can I help you?"

"Jody, this is Meredith Gardner. I'm so glad to catch you in the office on a Saturday; I need to speak with Attorney Reagan, it's an emergency."

"Mr. Reagan is doing some research at the courthouse right now. I'll have him return your call as soon as he gets back. I believe he said he'd be in the office by three."

"All right. Please ask him to contact me as soon as possible. Tell him that my husband Douglas is being held for questioning by the state police. I must speak to Mr. Reagan."

"Certainly, I'll send him a text to give him a head's up," Jody said, attempting to reassure me.

"Thank you. I appreciate it. I'll wait on his call."

I hung up the phone and absent mindedly petted Mittens as he hopped onto my lap. I sat at the desk, stared at the phone and knew that I had procrastinated long enough. Mittens purred and butted my hand with his head, seeking my attention.

"Have you been a good boy today?" I asked him as I rubbed the space between his ears and the bridge of his nose. His purring increased.

"Okay, I've got to do this." I dialed the phone number for Doug's parents and listened to the ring tone. The phone picked up after two rings.

"Hello," an enthusiastic voice boomed over the line.

"Hi Billy, this is Mommy. How you doin'?"

"Mommy! Nana, Johnny. . . Mommy's on the phone," he shouted excitedly, causing me to hold the receiver a few inches away from my ear. We definitely have to work on his inside voice versus outside voice.

I smiled to myself, I missed him. I missed both of my boys and can't believe that it was just two days ago when I worried about them sailing. It felt like they'd been gone for ages.

"Hello, Meredith?" a socially cultured voice spoke that needed no introduction.

"Hello Mother Gardner. I just wanted to call and check on the boys. Everything okay?"

"Yes, of course. What could be wrong?" my mother-in-law inquired stiffly.

"The boys can be a handful at times. But I'm sure they're enjoying their time with you. As a matter of fact, I was wondering if you would mind allowing them to stay another week? Something's come up; Doug and I will be tied up for a while." I know I sounded nervous and I prayed she wouldn't ask too many questions.

"Well, I suppose so. Are you and Douglas all right? You sound odd."

"Oh yes, we're fine. It would be a really big help though, knowing the boys are both being entertained and cared for. Would it be more convenient for you to have us drive up to retrieve them? Perhaps on the 30th of July," I suggested with a quick check of my calendar. God, I hope that would be enough time to get this mess resolved.

"Yes, that would suit perfectly. We do have a planned cruise we've scheduled for the following week, so I will need some time to pack for that."

"Absolutely. May I talk with Johnny and Billy for a minute?"

"Of course. One moment," she said as I heard her gently lay down the telephone receiver then a minute later, I listened to the sound of running footsteps.

"Mom," Johnny spoke first, "Nana said we're going to visit longer."

"Yes, that's right. Just one more week. Okay? Did you guys have a good time at Put-in-Bay?"

"Grandpop let me drive the boat. It was really cool. We spent the day exploring some caves and checking out a really tall monument. I forget the guy's name on it. Grandpop said there had been a big sea battle there," Johnny exclaimed.

"He's right, a huge battle with ships on Lake Erie in the War of 1812. You must have visited Perry's Monument on the island. We'll have to find some books in the library all about it when you get home," I said. It was reassuring to hear the excitement in my son's voice.

"Lemme talk," I could hear Billy complain to his older brother.

"Billy," I called through the telephone. "Don't fight with your brother or give your grandmother any trouble. Do you hear me?"

"I'm being good. Honest," Billy said. "Nana makes us go to bed early and yesterday I had to eat broccoli," he whispered into the mouthpiece. I could just imagine him trying to be secretive. His little whisper still boomed loudly.

"Okay. Promise me you'll listen to Nana and Grandpop and be good. Daddy and I will come up to get you in a week. I love you both and miss you. I'm sending you guys hugs and kisses."

"Bye Mom," they both shouted into the telephone before I heard the click.

No sooner had I hung up the phone, when it rang loudly. Hoping it was the attorney calling me back, I grabbed the receiver.

"Is it true? It's all over town that Doug was arrested," a breathless Aunt Fran inquired.

"Not arrested, just a person of interest being questioned," I tried to explain.

"Oh my God, we'll be right there," Aunt Fran replied anxiously.

The line went dead before I could say another word. I don't know who "we" meant, but I could guess. I went into the kitchen to start a pot of coffee, then laid out three mugs, spoons and dessert dishes on the counter. I was just taking a strawberry mousse out of the refrigerator when my aunt and Anna Thompson burst through the back door.

"Wow, you made it here in record time," I commented as each woman wrapped me in a fierce hug. Handbags dropped to the floor as they settled onto counter stools and stared at me expectantly.

"Well? Are you going to tell me what's going on? I know Doug is innocent of whatever it is he's being accused of, so what can we do?" Aunt Fran demanded.

Frances Andrews is my mother's sister and probably one of my best confidantes. She's an attractive woman; her dark blond hair streaked with a few gray strands, the only sign of her advancing years. She works out at the YWCA once a week and keeps busy running her dress shop, Frannie's Frocks. She and I look more like mother and daughter than my own mother and I; perhaps because we both have the same blond hair coloring and blue-gray eyes. I just wish I had her slimmer figure; mine tends to be a bit curvier and prone to packing on a few too many inches on thighs and hips – my curse.

I studied the two women as I poured hot coffee into mugs and served the strawberry mousse. Where do I begin?

"Y'all gonna tell us or not? I'm itchin' to know what all the fuss is about," drawled Anna in that Texan accent of hers that ranged from slightly southern to downright Texas cowhand.

Anna and her husband Chuck hailed from the Texas panhandle. When Chuck had to transfer with his job to Columbus or be forced to take an early retirement, the couple left the ranch and made the move to our rural, mid-Ohio community. Anna's son, Stevie, one of those change of life babies, is in my cub scout den and now Anna is a close friend of both me and my aunt. She may be twenty years my

56

senior, but we get along like sisters and I've always appreciated her company.

"It's just too horrible. I wish Sheriff Simmons would get back to town; he'd sort this out. That pompous state trooper is the problem. He's the one who took Doug in for questioning," I cried.

"Questioning on what? Can we start from the beginning? What's happened?" demanded Aunt Fran.

"Oh goodness, you don't know. Well, I suppose it began at the class reunion last night. Do you recall my old high school boyfriend, Bryan Kirkland?"

"Didn't he leave in your junior year? What's he got to do with this?" Aunt Fran asked.

"_Everything_," I groaned.

Chapter 7

Glancing between the two women, I waited to hear their thoughts. "So, you see, Doug is innocent of killing that girl or stabbing Bryan. We don't even know the gal's name."

"My goodness, what a story and what a mess," Aunt Fran murmured.

"You'll never forget this class reunion," remarked Anna.

"I already wish I could. I'm sorry we ever went."

"Mmm, this strawberry stuff is good," Anna said. "Sorry to ask at a time like this, but did you make this?" She swallowed another spoonful of the mousse, enjoying the cool summer dessert.

"Glad you like it, just Cool Whip and some strawberry Jello whipped together then fold in fresh berries and refrigerate. Easy," I told her as I scooted Mittens off one of the stools and claimed it for myself. He gave me a disgruntled look as he stalked away.

"My goodness, I can't believe you found another dead body. Just like last year when you found poor Mister Granger in the corn maze. I hope y'all are not going to make a habit of this," Anna exclaimed.

"Certainly not! I can't help it if dead bodies just pop up; it's not my fault," I cried in my defense.

"Do we know who this girl is, um, I mean, was?" asked Aunt Fran. "You say it's the same woman you met in the bathroom?"

"Pretty sure, I recognized her dress and flip-flop sandals, but I don't know what she was doing at the reunion or who she wanted to find."

"Well, I guess that's where we need to begin. We've got to identify this gal. We need a picture of her. Do you suppose Doc Stone will allow us to snap a photo of her face?" asked Aunt Fran as she set her coffee cup on the counter in a decisive gesture.

"You mean go visit the morgue?" squeaked Anna as she laid her spoon down in the empty dish. "Oh my gosh."

"Just pretend you're at the hospital. It'll be okay. We'll be in and out in a minute," stated Fran. "C'mon, let's go now before it gets any later."

She jumped up and grabbed Anna by the hand, propelling her out the door and toward the car. "We'll call you," she shouted to me as she slid behind the wheel and started the engine.

I stood by the kitchen door staring after them in amazement. Looks like my favorite partners in crime were on the case. Now, I need to focus my attention on speaking with Doug's lawyer and getting him home.

If thoughts could conjure people, just like ESP, my phone rang, and the caller ID showed Attorney Reagan on the line. I grabbed the receiver and answered quickly before the second ring.

"Mr. Reagan, thank you so much for returning my call."

"So, what's this all about? Your message said that Doug was in jail?" the lawyer asked.

"He's being held for questioning concerning the death of a woman at the Oak Meadow Inn. We found her body and now the state police think Doug is involved, which of course, is just ridiculous. He doesn't even know the woman and absolutely did not have anything to do with her death. You've got to do something!" I heard my voice become more strident with every word as my emotions bubbled to the surface.

"Well, Meredith, you do understand that I'm not a criminal attorney. I deal with family law. I can recommend someone, if you like."

"No, Doug asked me to call you. He trusts you."

"All right, calm down. I'll go straight over to the sheriff's office and speak to the officer in charge and Doug. See what I can do to get to the bottom of this. If he hasn't been formally charged, they can't hold him. Don't you worry now, we'll get this sorted out," reassured Reagan.

"Thank you so much. Should I meet you there? Do you need me to come?" I asked, chewing on my bottom lip.

"No. No need. I'll get your husband back home to you soon."

"Thank you again. I can't tell you how much I appreciate this."

Doctor Tom Stone laid down his scalpel and glanced toward the door as he heard rapid tapping on the glass. His face registered his surprise on seeing Fran Andrews and Anna Thompson staring through the window on the other side. Fran waved to him and gestured at the portal.

The doctor peeled off his rubber surgical gloves, draped a sheet over the body on his table, then leisurely strolled toward the door. He arched an eyebrow at the curious faces greeting him.

"Are you ladies lost?" he asked.

"Hello Tom. I wonder if I can ask a favor of you?" Fran asked with a sweet smile and tilt of her head as she tried to peer over his shoulder into the morgue examining room.

"Imagine that would depend upon the favor," he replied with a chuckle and waited expectantly. He studied the two women; Anna shrank backwards away from the entrance, but Fran craned her neck to see past him and took a step forward.

"Well, you see, Tom, I'm trying to help identify the young woman that was killed. If I could just get a little snapshot of her face, that's all I need, then I'll be out of your way."

"Uh huh, just a picture of her face. And who might you be helping, may I ask?"

"Well, um, Meredith of course and I suppose indirectly Doug Gardner. So that makes it really helping the sheriff's department, doesn't it?" Fran smiled and fluttered her eyelashes in a coy manner at the southern gentleman standing before her, hoping he wouldn't dismiss her.

"My, my. . . you do have a rather circumspect explanation. Am I to believe this tale?" He laughed then studied her solemn expression.

"It really is important. I must help my niece; you know Doug Gardner is innocent of any crime. What harm can it do to just get a photograph of the dead woman? We only want to ask around town to see if anyone recognizes her. C'mon, please Tom?" Fran tried again to wheedle her way with feminine wiles.

"All right. You can stop pleading your case. This is highly irregular. Give me your camera or whatever you're using, and I will take the picture. You wait right here. Do I make myself clear?" the doctor issued his decision.

Fran smiled sweetly and pressed a light kiss against his whisker stubbled cheek. She pulled out her cell phone from her purse, pressed the camera mode application, and handed it to the doctor.

"Thank you, Tom. I owe you one. Maybe stop by this weekend and I'll treat you to a home cooked meal," Fran offered.

"Harrumph," he muttered as he turned back to the draped table and carefully lowered the sheet to expose just the head and shoulders. He snapped two pictures then returned the cell phone to Fran. "I could get in trouble for this, you know. Don't tell anyone where you got that photograph."

"I won't, promise. You've been a big help. Thanks again, Tom." She waggled her fingers good-bye and linked her arm through Anna's as she hurried away down the hall and out the exit.

Once they were outside, Anna drew a deep breath and sigh of relief. "I swear, you could charm an ornery bull with that kind of sweet talk," Anna declared.

"Okay, so now what? Maybe we ought to print off that picture. I feel kind of funny having it on my phone. Let's pop into CVS drugstore and download the shot; print off a few copies," Fran decided as they headed toward town.

Chapter 8

Pacing the floor was no help. I needed to do something. But what? I finished loading the few dishes and mugs into the dishwasher and wiped off the breakfast bar out of habit then filled Mitten's bowl with fresh water. He rewarded me with a meow and loud purring; obviously he forgave my earlier transgressions. I gave him a short knuckle rub on the top of his head then resumed my pacing.

"What do you think Mittens? Maybe I should go down to the jail. What's taking so long to release Doug?"

"Mroww," Mittens rubbed his back against my legs. He circled me twice and butted his head alongside my ankle then gave up and wandered over toward the pet flap and outdoors where he could delight in scaring a bird or two.

I jumped at the sound of a soft tap on the kitchen door but relaxed when I saw that it was only Colleen.

"Hey, can I come in?" she asked as she closed the door and approached me.

"Please. . . I can't stand the silence around here; it's driving me crazy. I'm glad you're here," I admitted to my friend.

"How are you? Any news yet on Doug?"

"I'm waiting to hear back from our attorney. I spoke with him and he was heading over to the jail to talk with Doug and get him released. They can't hold him if he's not formally charged; at least I don't think so," I said.

"I wish there was something we could do. This is just crazy. Everything was fine until Bryan Kirkland came back into town and now look," Colleen declared in exasperation as she flounced onto a bar stool.

"I know, I know. If we could learn who that woman is, for starters, that would help. Why was she killed? Who was she waiting to see?"

"How do we go about researching her identity? Isn't that something the police will do with fingerprints or something?" Colleen asked. Her brow wrinkled in worry as she leaned on the counter and propped her chin on the heel of her hand.

"I suppose so, but if her fingerprints aren't on file some place, they'll come up empty anyway. Aunt Fran scooted out of here with a plan to get a picture of the woman. I haven't heard from her yet, but knowing my aunt, she won't give up until she does."

"Well, that's something. So, then what, we show her picture all around town?" Colleen asked.

"Yeah, why not? We've got to find someone who has seen this woman. She didn't appear out of nowhere. Somebody has to know her," I stated emphatically.

"Well, suppose we make a list of businesses or parts of town to visit and divide it up among us – canvass the entire area? I agree, we have to turn up some information."

"Okay, I feel a bit better now that we have a plan."

The words were no sooner out of my mouth when my aunt and Anna rushed through the kitchen door and excitedly waved an envelope at us. I swear, today my house felt like Grand Central Station.

"Got it!" exclaimed my aunt. "Tom Stone took the shot, but we're not supposed to tell anyone that's where we got the photograph."

She laid the envelope on the counter then ripped off the sealed edge and slid out a group of four-by-six-inch matte photos. She handed a picture to each of us. We all stared at the black and white image of the dead woman; I couldn't help trembling as I held the picture in my hand.

"Tomorrow, the four of us need to search for anyone who can recognize this gal. There's four of us, so let's divide up by the four compass points. Aunt Fran, you cover the south side of town. Anna, can you cover the eastern neighborhoods? Colleen will take the north and I'll do the west," I said.

"What do we do?" asked Anna nervously.

"Just show this picture to every neighbor, business owner, or anyone you meet and ask them if they've seen this woman before, and if they have, what's her name? Call me if any of you learn any information at all and I'll do the same. Agreed?"

"Okay. Operation photo ID it is," declared Aunt Fran as we all high-fived our hands in agreement as if we were members of James Patterson's Women's Murder Club. Let the sleuthing begin.

"Thank you. You know I love you all for doing this," I said with a hitch in my voice.

Colleen kissed me on the cheek and left with her copy of the photo in hand. Anna and Fran each hugged me then hurried out of the house just as a familiar, and oh so welcome, figure filled the doorway.

I ran to my husband and jumped into his arms. Doug lifted me off my feet as he embraced me in an emotional hug and demanding kiss. I clung to him and stroked the side of his face, feeling the rough whiskers along his jawline.

"Thank God you're home. I was frantic with worry."

"Reagan pointed out to that jerk Blackburn that he couldn't hold me without any evidence. But I am on suspension from work pending further investigation. Looks like you're stuck with me at home for a few days," Doug said with a resigned smile and nuzzled my neck.

"Just hold me, we'll figure out how to solve this mess later."

Chapter 9

Sunday felt far from peaceful. My mind spun in turmoil; my nerves were stretched as taut as a guitar string. I stared at Doug as he walked into the kitchen, dressed in old jeans and a faded t-shirt, then he rummaged through the laundry room cabinet. I heard him mumbling to himself, "Where's that large sponge?"

"What are you doing?" I asked him, my coffee cup suspended in mid-air between my mouth and the table.

"I'm gonna wash the car. Might as well do something useful with my free time," he replied calmly.

"Wash the car. . . just like that. Don't you think you should work on clearing your name? What do you plan on doing about that?" I snapped.

"I can't very well be sticking my nose into an investigation being run by the state police, now can I? Did you forget I'm on suspension? Actually, I planned on getting in a few holes of golf later today; after Tony finishes his shift. Thought the two of us would try the links at Oak Meadow."

"Uh huh, and here I thought you didn't enjoy playing golf. Could there be an ulterior motive for visiting Oak Meadow?"

"Now why would you think that? All I plan on doing is to spend a bit of time with my fellow coworker and enjoy the greens," Doug replied with a wink.

I gave him a knowing smile and a nod. Well, if he was going to be gone for part of the afternoon, I guess there was no reason I couldn't spend my time calling upon some of my Avon customers. Perhaps while I'm at it, I might just ask if anyone recognizes a certain picture too. I have to do something, or I'll bust. I can't get into trouble for just visiting my customers, now, can I?

Two hours later, Doug had hung up the water hose, put away his bucket and soap then went into the house to shower and change clothes. He came downstairs dressed in shorts and a knit polo shirt with a baseball cap on his head.

"How do I look? Will I pass for belonging to the country club set?" he asked.

"Hmm, you'll do." I smiled at him and waggled my fingers goodbye as I sipped my coffee and pretended to browse through the Sunday newspaper.

I waited until Doug had driven away before I grabbed my Avon tote bag packed with the latest campaign brochures and a few packaged orders ready for delivery. I hurried out of the house. Hopefully, I'll be able to catch some folks home on a Sunday afternoon. I didn't normally pester people on the Sabbath, but today I was making an exception.

I usually enjoy visiting with neighbors and friends as I walk my Avon sales' route in Meadowood. Delivering new campaign books, taking orders from customers, trying on new fragrances and cosmetics was all part of the job, plus I got to listen to the latest gossip in town. Cosmetic sales gave me my own personal income and a sense of independence; I didn't have to feel guilty about splurging on a new pair of shoes or treating myself to a salon visit if I used money that I had earned with my sales and not the household budget. Besides, it was fun.

Today more than ever, I needed to check in with my customers and pick their brains for ideas about our mystery woman. Someone must have seen her about town, and I planned on finding out who.

It was mid-afternoon and my feet were hurting while my bladder felt like bursting from too many hospitable cups of coffee or glasses of iced tea. I said goodbye to Carol Goodwin and made my way toward Teresa Maxwell's home on Walnut Street. I'd have to make Teresa my last stop. After stopping at fifteen houses and finding only ten of my customers at home, I was beginning to think this plan would not work.

Teresa Maxwell owned the beauty shop Cut & Curl. She's been styling my hair for the past eight years; I know she'll scold me when she sees the state of my short locks today. I love Teresa for her good-natured manner even though her appearance can be disarming when you meet her. Teresa believes in experimenting with every new hair color or style on herself before offering it to a customer. Some days her hair is flaming red or orange and other days you may find her with streaks of purple among her light brown strands. She dressed younger than her forty-five years but somehow that works for her. She also can be a huge gossip and today I was counting on those very qualities to help me in my quest.

I pressed the doorbell and waited patiently for Teresa to open the door of her quaint cottage. I didn't have to wait long.

"Hello!" Teresa's voice boomed in greeting as she welcomed me into her home. She wore a long flowing caftan with a wild floral pattern that matched her shocking pink hair color.

"Hi Teresa. I've got your Avon order if you have a few minutes?"

"Sure thing sweetie, come on in. My goodness gal, what did you do to that hair of yours? I can tell at a glance you're not using the conditioner I gave you."

I grimaced. I knew I'd hear a lecture on my hair. "I know, I've been in a rush the last few days."

"Well, you stop by the shop this week and I'll give you a deep conditioning treatment; that'll put the shine back into that dull hair. You can use a bit of a trim too," Teresa offered.

"I'll do that. So how have you been?" I asked politely as I rummaged through my tote bag to find her order. "Here you go." I placed the sealed bag on the table.

"Want some iced tea?" Teresa asked as she ripped open the paper sack and placed the contents in front of her.

"Would you mind if I use your restroom first?"

"No of course not. Just down the hall. I'll look over my goodies."

"Thanks. I really appreciate it."

When I returned, Teresa was nose deep into the new sales brochure and jotting down selections of nail polish. She looked up and smiled as I sat back down.

"You look tuckered out. Been a long day?" she asked then jumped up to retrieve two tall glasses of iced tea with lemon wedges perched on the glass rim. "This should perk you up."

"Thanks. I've been out all afternoon. I'm sorry to bother you on a Sunday, but I just didn't want to wait until your shop was open tomorrow," I started to explain.

"Sounds serious; wait on what?"

I drew the photograph out of my bag and laid it in the center of the table. "Have you seen this woman? Maybe she's been in the shop?"

Teresa picked up the photograph and stared at it. Her mouth opened then shut again as she raised questioning eyes to mine. "Um, ah, is this a morgue photo? Oh, my goodness, Merry." Teresa shuddered.

"Mm-hmm, that's the problem. This gal was killed Friday night, and no one knows who she is. Can you take another look? Does she appear at all familiar?" I asked, pointing at the pale face.

Teresa studied the picture then slid it back to me. "I think she may have come into the shop. I remember a woman, real shy and quiet like, just needed a haircut. Might be her."

"Do you recall her name?"

"No, sweetie, I don't. Come to think of it I don't believe she told me her name. Yes, that's right. I remember now. She paid in cash too."

"Oh dear, guess I had my hopes up you would know her. So many people around town come through Cut & Curl; I thought for sure I'd learn her name at least."

"Is this woman involved in the story going around town about Doug being in jail? Did he have something to do with her death?" whispered Teresa, although we were alone in her kitchen.

"Doug's not in jail. The police questioned him because we found the body, that's all. Remember my class reunion party being held Friday night at Oak Meadow Inn? I saw this gal at the Inn during the reunion, then we found her, um, body on Saturday morning when we were cleaning up from the party. Of course, Doug had nothing to do with it. We were just first on the scene," I stated.

"Gee, I'm sorry I can't be more help," then Teresa laughed and patted my hand, "You sure do find a lot of dead bodies."

I gritted my teeth as I replied, "That's what everyone keeps telling me. I don't plan it that way."

"No, I don't imagine you do. So hey, Merry, can you order me two bottles each of these colors? You know I could buy salon polish, but honestly, this Avon lasts just as long as the more expensive brands and my customers like all the shades," she said as she handed me her scribbled list.

"Okay, I'll have them in about two weeks. Thanks Teresa. I've got to be going. I'll call the shop tomorrow to make an appointment for that treatment and cut."

"You do that. Such pretty hair as yours needs to be pampered."

Most of the regulars at the Oak Meadow golf course play in early morning so by mid-afternoon, the links contained only a small group of players spread out across the nine holes. Doug and Tony hefted their rented golf club bags over their shoulders as they strolled toward the third hole.

"Do we appear to be a pair of cheap amateurs since we aren't riding around in one of those silly golf carts like those old codgers up ahead?" Doug asked. He paused to watch the men tee off.

Tony snorted then glanced quickly over his shoulder as he replied sheepishly, "I don't have the faintest idea of what I'm doing. You sure no one will suspect us?"

"Why, we're only playing a round of golf, deputy Dalton. Two old friends enjoying the sunshine, that's all," Doug said with a chuckle.

"Yeah right," snorted Tony. He slammed his driver into the turf once more, missing the tiny white ball altogether. He grimaced and continued to look guilty.

"You could at least pretend you're enjoying the game," admonished Doug. He forcefully drove his ball toward a clump of trees at the perimeter of the course. "Oops."

They grabbed their bags and sauntered across the lush lawn as they followed the direction of the wayward golf balls. Both men made a big show of searching the tall grass and undergrowth within the copse in case anyone was watching, then ducked behind the trees out of sight. Doug and Tony propped up their golf bags against a wide tree trunk, to be retrieved later. They stealthily made their way through the trees toward the rear of the inn. Doug had recalled the delivery entrance of the building and the line of trees that shielded the refuse dumpsters from view; wouldn't want smelly garbage to be seen by club members on the course. Now that policy would work in their favor.

"You sure about this?" asked Tony.

"Yeah, c'mon. We need another look at the scene before any trace evidence is totally gone. You gonna let those troopers run roughshod over you? They could have missed something. They're not God, you know, just because they're state."

"You're right. No reason for us to back off just because Blackburn thinks the state police are in charge," Tony admitted.

They stepped into the clearing and quickly glanced around to ensure no workers lingered outside. Doug and Tony both tugged off their leather gloves, stuffed them into pockets then slipped on a pair of rubber surgical gloves. Doug motioned Tony to search on the left while he crept to the right, poking among the grass, under shrubbery, looking for anything that didn't belong there.

Doug stopped and waved to Tony to join him as he stared at the heavy iron dumpster. Torn crime scene tape dangled from one end. He pointed to the wheel marks on the ground.

"This has been moved. It's been pushed to the left from where it sat yesterday morning," Tony stated.

"Exactly." Doug silently lifted the lid and peered over the side. "Empty. Appears the garbage men came by. We're not going to find anything inside now."

"Now what?" Tony asked as he glanced over his shoulder and around the vacant lot.

"Hey. . . check out underneath this thing. See that glint? There. Just behind that back wheel," Doug said as he crouched down and tried to reach underneath.

"Let me try. I've got long pants on. I can crawl better than you can," Tony offered as he got onto hands and knees to inch his way closer to the bottom of the container. He slid his hand along the ground until his fingers grasped a hard object.

"Be careful. If it's what I think it is, you don't want to risk cutting yourself."

"Got it!" Tony slowly backed up and got to his feet, gripping his prize. "I think we just found the murder weapon," Tony exclaimed excitedly.

A long slender blade about seven inches long with a steel hilt lay in the deputy's palm. Dried blood stained the long knife.

"The killer must have tossed the knife into the dumpster but in the dark he probably didn't see that he had missed, and it fell onto the ground, hidden from view until the container was moved," Doug surmised. "Bring any evidence bags?"

"No. Did you?"

"No. Let's see if we can borrow a zipped food storage bag from the kitchen. You'll have to ask; I'm not supposed to be here, remember."

"Okay." Tony and Doug walked toward the outside kitchen door and entered the building.

The two men startled a young lad up to his elbows in sudsy dish water. "Hey, you can't come in here. Employees only."

"It's all right. We're with the sheriff's office. I just need to borrow one of your plastic bags. Where can I find one?" asked Tony as he pulled his ID from his pocket and flashed his badge at the young boy.

"Over there, bottom cabinet," directed the boy grudgingly.

The swinging door separating the cooking area from the rear kitchen and prep room opened with a bang as Ricardo strode into the room. One glance at the two men rummaging through one of his cabinets raised his ire.

"May I ask what you think you are doing?" he demanded.

"Just need a zip lock baggie, that's all." Tony said as he shook out a bag and with a flourish unzipped it and slid the bloody weapon into it for safe keeping.

Ricardo stared at the bag and its contents. "That's my chef knife. Where did you get it?"

"You're saying this knife belongs to you?" Doug questioned softly, stepping forward.

"Well, yes. See here; I have one missing." Ricardo pointed to a case of varying sized knives all perfectly lined up with an empty slot between a short paring knife and a serrated edge bread knife.

"When was the last time you used the chef knife? Why didn't you report it missing on Saturday morning when you gave your statement?"

Ricardo suddenly realized the depth of trouble that he was in and what the bloody knife implied. His face drained of color, and he gulped twice as he glanced between the two men.

"I had nothing to do with the death of that woman. I don't know who took my knife. Anyone could have picked it up; it was lying on the table right here. I used it to carve the roast chickens, then must have set it down when I got busy with the next dish."

"You're sure?" Doug asked.

"We're going to need you to come down to the sheriff's office and make a formal statement," Tony told the chef.

Ricardo slowly sank into a chair. His hands shook as he nodded in agreement.

"Let's get this to forensics. I doubt they can still pick up any fingerprints, but they'll need to test the blood to see if it's a match to our victim or anyone else," Doug stated.

"He's right, you know; anyone could have taken that knife from the kitchen," Tony said as they made their way through the tree line to retrieve their discarded golf clubs. They'd had enough golf for one day; but it had served its purpose.

"Including me?" asked Doug, pausing in his tracks.

"Um, uh, I didn't say that," stammered Tony.

Chapter 10

Mittens meowed and rubbed his back against my legs as he performed his usual dance, circling me two or three times while I tried to walk across the kitchen floor.

"C'mon boy, give me a break; you've got fresh water and food in your bowl. I know it's not your favorite flavor, but it was on sale."

"Mroww," Mittens replied with a swish of his tail as he defiantly headed to his cat flap and outdoors to torment some unsuspecting bird or insect.

I stirred scrambled eggs in the frying pan and retrieved English muffins from the toaster just as the microwave bell signaled the sizzling strips of bacon were ready. As skilled as any short-order cook, I plated our breakfasts in a jiffy and carried them to the table. Chilled glasses of orange juice sat on the pretty floral placemats waiting to be drunk; I poured two steaming mugs of coffee then plopped down to enjoy my hot morning meal, a rare treat for me.

"Breakfast is ready," I shouted up the stairs to my husband. His food will be cold if he waits much longer but I indulged myself. "Mmm, this is good. So, these are what hot eggs taste like?" I chuckled to myself as I gobbled another forkful.

Doug wiped the sleep from his eyes as he stumbled down the stairs and reached for the life-saving mug of hot coffee. He took an appreciative sip before settling onto the bar stool at the counter.

"Thanks Babe. Why'd you let me sleep so late?"

"Figured you needed it. You tossed and turned half the night and I know you've not been getting much sleep lately. Maybe breathing in all that nice fresh air yesterday while on the golf course helped you relax." I ate another forkful of food before continuing, "How many holes did you and Tony actually play?"

Doug snorted and threw me a knowing look, "Technically three, but I think we may have damaged the turf more than anything. Tony hit the ground instead of the golf ball on most shots. It served its purpose though."

"How so?"

"We managed to crawl around that dumpster again unseen, behind the building and found the murder weapon."

"Really! Are you sure? You found a bloody knife? What did it look like? What did you do with it? Why didn't you tell me last night?"

"My, my; so many questions. You aren't getting involved in this, are you? Because I don't want you and your friends getting into trouble. That's why I didn't mention finding the knife," Doug said.

"Of course not, you know I wouldn't do that," I replied with my fingers crossed behind my back.

"That's the problem; I know you would and probably will. Anyway, we found a long chef's knife and Tony bagged it and took it into forensics for testing."

"A chef knife. . . did it belong to Ricardo? Did you speak to him yesterday?" I asked. My curiosity made me forget my delicious breakfast rapidly growing cold.

"Yeah, Tony and I spoke to him. He claimed the knife as his, but of course he had no idea who took it, how it got outside and naturally says he had nothing to do with the murder. I think I actually believe him. He says he laid the knife on the prep table; anyone could have picked it up."

"So, we're back to square one. We don't know who stabbed Bryan or killed that poor woman. Do the police even know who she is?" I asked, chewing on a cold piece of bacon. I sipped my coffee thoughtfully, my head spun with unanswered questions and speculations.

"Truthfully, I don't know what Blackburn knows at this point. I'm being kept out of it, still suspended. Of course, that doesn't mean I can't have a conversation with a friend or two, even have dinner at Oak Meadow Inn. It's still a free country," Doug stated.

The ringing of the telephone interrupted my next question. I reached for the phone and saw my aunt's number on the caller ID.

"Operation Photo ID is on," whispered Fran.

"Hi, Aunt Fran. How are you?" I answered loudly and smiled at my husband, indicating who was on the phone. I grabbed my coffee mug and waved to Doug as I stepped outside onto the deck. Mittens was close on my heels. I sat down on one of the patio chairs to resume my conversation out of ear shot.

"Can you get away?" Aunt Fran asked excitedly.

"Yeah, I think so. What's up?"

"Come down to the shop. I can't leave the store unattended and today is Betty's day off. The girls will be here; we've got news."

"Okay. I'll be right down," I agreed and hung up.

I watched Mittens leap onto a green grasshopper, then release it and catch him again. I swear, that cat loved to torment his victims. I left him outside and returned to the kitchen, placed my mug in the sink and gathered up the remnants of the breakfast dishes. I quickly packed the dishwasher then grabbed my purse.

"Aunt Fran needs my help at the shop; she's alone today. I won't be long. I told her I'd lend a hand," I informed Doug with one hand on the doorknob.

"Go ahead. Maybe I'll work on cleaning out the garage or something."

Within minutes I was running into Frannie's Frocks to join Anna Thompson, Colleen Callahan and my Aunt Fran. The three of them wore identical expressions. Excitement, apprehension, and satisfaction all flitted across their faces as they peered at the black and white photo of the dead woman.

"You all look like you've won the lottery," I said as I approached my fellow conspirators.

"Wait until you hear what Martha Parker told Anna. She's seen our mystery woman," exclaimed my aunt, her eyes twinkled, and a grin spread across her face as wide as a child's on Christmas morning.

"Wonderful. Oh, hey, I showed the picture to Teresa Maxwell yesterday, you know how everyone in town goes to Cut & Curl so I figured she might know the gal. Teresa said she did come in for a haircut, but she didn't know her name and the gal paid in cash so there's no credit card receipt to follow up on. Hope you had better luck," I told them.

"Well, Martha examined the photograph and remembers the woman coming into the bakery. She didn't know her name, but she did remember that the gal wore a blue gingham waitress uniform. Isn't that great? Martha told me she thought it was odd for someone who worked in a restaurant to be buying her baked goods. Why not just get a dessert where you worked?" Anna studied the faces of her friends expectantly, watching for their reactions to this earth-shattering news. Not seeing the excitement that she was feeling, she continued, "Anyway, we don't have that many eating joints around here; we ought to be able to figure out which place wears a blue gingham uniform," stated Anna.

"You're right, we don't have a wide selection of restaurants. Let's make a list," I said.

Colleen pulled out her day planner from her purse; ever the schoolteacher always prepared. She tapped a pencil on a blank note page and waited expectantly.

"Let's start with Oak Meadow Inn, they've got three dining venues, but I don't think any of their wait staff wear blue check," Aunt Fran said as Colleen wrote.

"We can rule out Martha's bakery and deli. Oh, how about the Cracker Barrel out on highway twenty-six? No, they use those brown aprons, don't they?" Anna speculated.

"Well, there's Jack's Racks barbeque place over on West Elm Street. What do their servers wear? Maybe she worked there," I said as I looked questioningly between my friends.

"Hmm, let me think a minute. Sam Tilley and I had supper there once; I sure miss that man. Let me see, if I could just recall. . . No, I can picture our waitress in my head now, she was a cute little college gal and wore red and white stripes. I remember thinking she looked like she ought to be in a hospital, you know, like those candy-stripers," Aunt Fran said.

"Well, we're not making much progress. Where else? Has to be nearby for her to do her business in Meadowood. What's the name of that diner, the one that looks like an old railway car, over on Pottstown road?" I asked.

"Oh, I know the one you mean. Chuck and I stopped by for a bite on the way home from Columbus a couple weeks ago. I think I told you about going to chat with that HR person at Chuck's company. Chuck wanted me to hear what kind of retirement benefits he can get if he retires next winter. We were there a lot longer than I thought and had missed lunch, so on the way home we stopped for some coffee and pie," drawled Anna. "I don't know the name of that little place, but it did look like a cute train car. I wouldn't mind goin' back for another piece of their delicious apple pie."

"Anyone feel like a drive?" I asked. "We've listed all the restaurants in our area. Now if she worked closer to Columbus, we're in trouble because there are hundreds of places. What do you think?"

Colleen finished her notation and closed her planner. "Well, I'm game if you are. Let's go now."

"Yes, let's go. Road trip," declared Anna as she clapped her hands.

"Well, I can't leave the store, but you three check out the place. Take lots of pictures and see what you can find out. I'll wait to hear from you," Aunt Fran said.

"Okay. Let me give Doug a call to tell him I'll be home later," I said as I pressed the quick dial for home on my cell phone. It rang a few times before I heard my husband's voice. "Hi honey. I'm going to be home later than I planned. Anna and Colleen are here and we're sorting through some stuff. Okay?"

"Sure. I'm busy in the garage. Hey, did you know we have a box of baby crap out there? You don't want to keep that stuff, do you? I could use the room," Doug said.

"Just set it aside and I'll look at it when I get home. Maybe we can donate it to a woman's shelter or something. I'm certainly not planning on using it again." I disconnected the call and nodded to Anna and Colleen. "I didn't lie, not really. We are sorting through some stuff. Now, who wants to drive?"

Chapter 11

In the end, we decided that Anna would drive her Jeep since she was the only one who had visited the diner before and knew where it was located. Colleen rode in the back seat while I took the shot gun position up front. The weather made for a pleasant day to take a short ride; sunny and warm, but not too hot. It was early enough for us to avoid any busy lunch crowd too; maybe we'll find a chance to talk with some of the staff.

Anna drove westward out of town, following the county road until it turned onto State Route 20. We passed the medical center and hospital. My thoughts turned toward my recent visit with Bryan; I wondered how he was, and for that matter, where he was.

"Has anyone seen Bryan Kirkland around town?" I asked Colleen and Anna. "Do you think he's staying at his father's house?"

"Haven't seen him in town but it would make sense that he'd be home. Wouldn't it? I imagine he has to sort through his father's personal papers. Usually so much to do following a death," Colleen commented.

"Still, after all the hub-bub with the reunion and his injury. . . what's he up to?" My mind kept niggling at that image of his bare shoulder, tugging at some hidden recollection that I couldn't quite grasp. It'll come to me later.

Anna turned off the state route and followed a winding two-lane road through the rural countryside. Fields of wildflowers in riots of color marked our path while tall grasses swayed across the gently rolling hillside; groups of dairy cows stood chewing contentedly as we passed. Ahead of us, a horse-drawn black buggy clip-clopped along; within, members of an Amish family peacefully rode home from marketplace or perhaps their meeting house. Anna slowed our car as the buggy pulled over toward the berm to allow us to pass safely. We waved to the children dressed in their cute bonnets and smocks.

"Could you live like that?" asked Colleen, pointing to the Amish family.

"Probably not. I'm too spoiled by all my modern conveniences. Afraid I like my electricity too much," I said.

"I envy them their deep faith and simple way of life, though," Colleen said as she watched the buggy turn down a long narrow lane.

"Honey, you don't need to be Amish to have a deep faith," drawled Anna. "As for a simple life, we can all seek that. Just eliminate the unimportant stuff and look deep inside yourself to discover what's really meaningful."

We rode on, each silent with our own thoughts, considering Anna's words. Fifteen minutes later, Anna pulled the jeep into a wide gravel parking lot next to a faded red and yellow train car. A rusted metal sign hung on a bracket above the roof and proclaimed the place as Hank's Erie Caboose Diner. Gray dust swirled around us as we came to a stop and parked to the right of the eating establishment. Several eighteen wheelers parked side by side in the open lot and along the roadway.

"My dad always said the truckers know the best places to eat," I commented as we walked toward the entrance and pushed open the screen door.

"Let's go check it out," said Colleen as we entered and waited on someone to seat us.

A middle-aged woman with salt and pepper gray hair and a friendly smile hustled past us carrying a tray loaded with dishes. "Be right with you gals," she said as she hurried toward a back table.

I poked Colleen in the side as I nodded toward the server with her stained white apron tied around the waist of a blue and white gingham dress.

"This has to be the place," I whispered.

"How about this booth?" asked the bedraggled waitress.

"Fine," I answered for all of us. Colleen and I slid into one side while Anna took the seat across from us.

The waitress tossed down three dog-eared menus covered with a clear plastic laminate. "What can I get you to drink?"

"Coffee," we all answered then smiled.

She hurried to slip behind the tall counter, grabbed a full pot of coffee off the machine, stopped to pour hot refills for two of the men seated at the counter and returned to us, juggling three ceramic mugs in one hand. With precision from long practice, the waitress placed a mug in front of each of us and poured the steaming brew.

"What can I get you? We're still serving breakfast if that's what tickles your appetite, or Hank can fire up the grill for burgers and dogs." She reached for the pencil that was tucked behind her ear and grabbed an order pad from her apron pocket, then glanced expectantly between us.

"I'd really like one of those delicious looking cinnamon rolls I see in the case," I ordered.

"Have any of your apple crumb pie on hand?" asked Anna. "I had that the last time I was here. Mmm, so good."

"May I have one of your blueberry muffins?" asked Colleen.

"Sure thing. Coming right up," the server said as she rushed off to get our treats. She was back in less than three minutes.

"Looks like this place does quite a business," I commented to her as she placed the dessert plates in front of us.

"You betcha, and you've come at our slow time of day. We stay busy most of the time," she remarked.

"I can imagine. Must be difficult keeping up with only one waitress on duty," I said as I looked around. There were three cooks manning the griddles visible behind the short wall separating the counter space from the kitchen, but I didn't see any other servers.

"Sure is. We had another gal, but she hasn't shown up for work in a few days and ole Hank hasn't bothered to hire a replacement yet."

I shot a questioning glance at Anna and Colleen and received their slight nods to continue.

"Um, ah, Margie," I addressed our waitress, reading the plastic name tag pinned to her uniform. "Could you look at this photo and maybe tell me if you recognize the girl?" I withdrew the picture from my purse and carefully slid it across the table toward the waitress.

Her puzzled look turned to one of shock as she stared at the morgue photograph. "Oh my God! No, it can't be. . ."

"Can you tell us her name? Did she work here?" Colleen asked softly.

"Maybe you better sit down, honey," Anna suggested as she scooted closer to the wall on the bench seat, opening a space.

Margie sunk onto the booth seat. "That's Hilda Moran. Yes, she worked here. I haven't seen her since she finished work Thursday night. She didn't show up for her weekend shifts; Hank figured she must have run off with that trucker friend of hers."

I raised an eyebrow, and Anna and Colleen exchanged surprised glances at this piece of news.

"Has she worked here long? She from around these parts?" I inquired.

"What? No, um, she's only been here about two months, I guess. Just dropped in one day, looking for work. What happened to her?" Margie asked as she stared at the photo again.

"I'm really sorry. I only met her briefly, but she seemed like a nice gal. She was, um, murdered Friday night outside of Meadowood," I said.

Anna softly patted the server's hand and pressed a paper napkin into her other as a tear slowly trickled down Margie's cheek.

"Do you know where she was staying? Did she live nearby?"

"I think she rented a room from that extended stay motel down the road; can't remember the exact name of the place. It's not much to look at but Hilda said it was cheap enough and that's all she cared about," Margie said as she wiped her eyes.

Suddenly, the diner's screen door slammed loudly as a large man stormed into the restaurant and stood searching the long narrow room. His gaze fell on Margie and he moved toward us.

"Oh my God, it's Big Jim Johnson," Margie whispered, then hastened to stand to meet the approaching man.

"Where's my gal? Where's Hildie?" the man's voice boomed and ricocheted off the walls of the tin diner.

"Hey there, Big Jim. How y'all doing today?" Margie greeted the giant and ushered him into an empty booth. She quickly set a mug of hot coffee before him. "Want the usual?"

"I don't see Hildie. Where is she?" he demanded again.

"She's not here, Big Jim. Now, you just drink some of that coffee and I'll get a plate of food right out for you. There're some folks over there that will want to talk with you a might." Margie nodded and pointed to the women listening intently.

I shuddered as I studied the massive man squeezed into the narrow booth. He must weigh at least three hundred pounds while his baseball capped head came close to brushing the seven-foot-tall ceiling of the diner. He wore a pair of faded blue jeans with a dingy yellow t-shirt barely long enough to tuck into his waistband. I swear I didn't think they made shoes that size; his feet appeared to be wearing small canoes.

I wondered if investigating by ourselves was such a good idea after all. My burst of bravery was dissolving into a spasm of foolishness. I'd feel a whole lot safer if Doug were by my side now and he was the one questioning this Paul Bunyan giant. There's no way the three of us women could handle this man if he became upset when he learns of Hilda's fate. I swallowed hard, considering my options and just how much detail I should divulge and what his reactions will be.

"Can we leave?" asked Colleen nervously with a nod toward the big man stuffing his face.

"I don't see how," Anna stated.

"Don't you want to learn more about this Hilda? It's obvious he was devoted to the woman. We must speak with him," I insisted.

"He scares me," admitted Colleen.

"Me too," whispered Anna.

"I know what you mean; just the look of him is scary," I said.

The silverware on our table rattled as the floor shook beneath the heavy footsteps of the enormous man. He towered over us as he looked questioningly at the three of us. His massive frame stood there, waiting for one of us to speak.

"Hello," I said in a shaking voice then tried to instill more confidence in my tone. "Can we chat with you about your friend Hilda?"

"You know my Hildie?" he asked, his eyes darting hopefully back and forth between us.

"Um, well, I think I may have met her a few days ago. She seemed like a very nice woman, pretty too."

"Where's my Hildie? You know where she is? She promised me she'd wait for me," he said, the volume of his voice lower now but still caused me to wince.

"How long have you and Hilda been together?" I dared to ask.

"Couple of months. Met her outside Barstow; gave her a ride 'cross country in my rig. We hit it off right away, but she was pining for some dude back east."

"So, you're a trucker?" I asked.

"That's my rig out front, been on the road for thirteen years. Hildie is gonna come truckin' with me."

"Did Hilda say the fella she knows lives around here? Do you know his name?" I continued my inquiry.

"Nah, he's dead. Some Army dude she hooked up with out west. She just wanted to see where he lived, so she could kinda say goodbye. That's why she hitched a ride with me from California to here."

"Big Jim, may I call you that? My name's Meredith Gardner; these are my friends Anna and Colleen. Er, Big Jim, is this your friend Hilda?" I held up the photograph and watched his face crumple as he stared at the dead woman.

Pools of tears filled his eyes and ran down his cheeks. He pulled a wrinkled red bandana from a back pocket and used it to mop the wetness then loudly blew his nose into the cloth. I watched him as he pressed the photograph against his chest then raised his eyes to me.

"What happened to my Hildie?"

"I'm so sorry for your loss. I hate to tell you this, but she was stabbed late Friday night. The police are searching for her killer. That's really all I know. We didn't even know her name until we came here," I stated. Colleen and Anna remained silent as we watched the gentle giant mourn his lost love.

"I had a run to New York. Hildie told me she was gonna come into some big money and when I got back, she was leaving with me. We had it all planned; we were gonna be a team," Big Jim explained. His shoulders shook as he controlled silent sobs. "I wanna see her. Where is she?" he demanded as he reined in his emotions.

"You'll have to ask the sheriff's department in Meadowood. They can take you to the morgue. That's where she is now. They might be able to tell you more," I told him. I really did feel sorry for his pain.

Big Jim turned and tossed some dollars down on the counter for Margie then slowly left, his feet dragging as the door closed silently behind him. We listened to the sounds of his diesel engine fire up and the crunch of tires as he pulled out and headed down the road toward Meadowood.

"Whew, I've been holding my breath the entire time," Colleen said in relief.

"That poor, poor man. I wonder what he'll do now," said Anna.

"At least we've identified the dead woman and we know how long she's been in Ohio and where she came from," I stated. "Big Jim said she came to see the home of a dead soldier. She was pining for some guy who was in the Army; isn't that what he said?"

"Who do we know in this area that served and died in the military this past year? I can't think of anyone. The Miller's son joined the Navy after graduation last June but he's okay; his mother showed me a picture of him on his ship docked in Norfolk, Virginia just the other day," Colleen said.

"Gosh I wish he could have told us more. Maybe Margie might remember something Hilda told her about this soldier."

The waitress seated two other customers before stopping at our table and handed us our bill; she paused as she considered whether or not to say more to us. I could see the hesitation on her face.

"Thanks a bunch for being so kind to Big Jim. He's really just a big Teddy bear; his size frightens most folks. He took it pretty hard about Hilda dying. I knew he would. He had it bad for her," Margie said.

"Margie, did Hilda ever mention to you about some soldier she knew out in California that died but he was from around these parts? Jim said Hilda wanted to see his home or something. Wonder if she ever said who he was?" I asked.

Margie thought for a minute, "Once, I recall her talking about this fella she loved but he got killed over in Iraq. His family was well to do, lived in a fancy mansion. I don't know if any of that was true or she was just spinning a tale. Hilda lied when it suited her. As for her coming into some money, that might be a tall tale too. Hank almost fired her on the spot a couple weeks ago when he caught her fingers in the till. He warned her not to steal from him again."

"Thanks Margie, you've been a big help," I said.

96

"I've got to get back to work; lunch crowd is comin' in and we're getting swamped. You gals take care now and come back."

"You too," I told her with a smile, and I meant it.

"Ladies, I think we need to head home. I don't believe we're going to learn any more information today," Colleen declared.

"I promised Aunt Fran we'd take pictures and I plum forgot. Let me at least snap one inside the diner and maybe one of Margie."

I managed to click several shots with my cell phone camera while Colleen and Anna paid our bill. We left a generous tip on the table for Margie then paused outside to capture one more photo of the unique railcar diner before climbing into Anna's Jeep for the ride home. Our road trip had proven fruitful indeed but left more questions to be answered. Maybe Hilda's lodging room could provide more clues. Did we dare? Perhaps later.

Chapter 12

After showing Aunt Fran the photographs of Margie and Hank's caboose, I hopped into my car where I had parked it near the shop and drove home. The rest of the afternoon found me hunched over several cardboard boxes filled with who knew what. Doug had piled anything he discovered in the garage into empty cartons that weren't so empty now. I sat on a lawn chair in the middle of the driveway surrounded by his efforts; sorting through our forgotten treasures, deciding which items I could discard, and which held memories too dear to lose.

The warm sunshine felt good on my face and shoulders. I chuckled out loud as I handled toys or baby clothes that had belonged to the boys. They were such sweet babies. I cuddled a worn Teddy bear, missing one glass eye and sporting a torn ear; he had been loved to death, poor thing. I just might keep him.

Mittens meowed his pleasure at being outside with his humans in sight; he stalked a sparrow that had been foolish enough to land on his turf then turned his attentions to stretching and rubbing his back against the warm deck boards. He was thoroughly enjoying the bright day.

Doug carried two tall glasses of lemonade as he stepped off the deck. He handed one to me then quirked his eyebrow in an expression I recognized all too well.

"What?" I asked, suspicious of that look.

"I just hung up the phone from talking with Tony down at the station. Seems some big dude came in inquiring about his girlfriend. Said her name was Hilda Moran and she happens to be our unidentified victim. Funny thing, he told Tony that he found out about her death from a group of women that he met in a diner over near Pottstown. You wouldn't know anything about that, would you?"

"Well, um, I might." I turned my attention back to the pile of clothes in front of me, hiding my guilty face.

"I thought you promised me you wouldn't get involved. You could have been in danger. You don't know who you're dealing with when you run off like that." Doug dragged his fingers through his hair and gave me one of his stern glares that he normally reserved for the boys. "What am I going to do with you? Honestly, Meredith, you can't go sticking your nose into police business."

"I wasn't, not really. All we did, Aunt Fran and the girls, I mean, was show the woman's picture around town to see if anyone knew her. We just wanted to learn her name, that's all. But when Martha told us she saw the gal in her shop one day, and she was wearing a blue gingham waitress uniform. . . well we just wanted to find out where she worked. And we did! She was a waitress at this cute little diner, really, it's an old railroad car. We showed the picture to a woman in the diner, and she told us Hilda's name. That's all we were doing. We had a coffee and some dessert and then we planned to leave."

"And just how did you manage to get a photograph of the deceased?"

"I can't say. We promised we wouldn't."

Doug shot me another look, clearly his patience was running thin, "What about talking to this strange man?"

"Oh well, yes, that would be Big Jim. He came in while we were eating our dessert. Margie, that's the waitress there, she sort of introduced us. But wait until I tell you, Big Jim's a trucker and he said Hilda hitched a ride with him from California all the way to Ohio. Isn't that interesting?" I couldn't keep the excitement out of my voice. "She told him she wanted to see the home of her dead lover. He was a soldier killed in Iraq. If that's true, then who was she planning to meet at the Inn that night? When I spoke to her in the ladies' room, she said she was meeting someone."

"I'll admit you girls, and your nosy grapevine, did better than the state police. Blackburn would still be searching for that gal's identity if not for your meddling."

"Do you think Big Jim had anything to do with her death? He seemed really upset; he cried and everything."

"According to Tony, the man's got trip tickets to vouch for his whereabouts. He drove his truck on a run to upstate New York on the dates in question, so he has an alibi. Blackburn can verify it with the weigh stations along the route."

"Good. I'd hate to think of him as a suspect. What's going to happen now?" I asked.

"I suppose after Doc Stone submits his official autopsy report and signs off on the death certificate, Hilda's body will be released to her kin or closest relation. That's likely to be this Big Jim. He told Tony he wanted Hilda to be cremated and he plans to carry her ashes with him on his truck, something about promising they would travel together," Doug said with a shake of his head.

"Oh, my goodness, that's so sweet but rather creepy, too. He told us they were a team and planned to ride that eighteen-wheeler of his across the country. I guess he still plans to do that." I closed my eyes as I imagined an urn propped on the seat of his cab. Ugh.

"Looks like we're back at the beginning," Doug mumbled, deep in thought. "Maybe we ought to do just that, let's go back where this all started. How'd you like to have dinner tonight at the Inn?"

"Lovely. Sounds like we aren't going there just for the food. What did you have in mind?" I asked.

"I need to see the place, take my time, walk through everyone's movements again in my mind. A piece of this puzzle doesn't fit; I can't quite put my finger on it. Maybe if we go back to Oak Meadow, I don't know. . . I'm hoping something, a clue, will jump out at me."

"It better hit you square in the chest, if we're going to clear your name and solve this mystery. I know you are innocent, but that Trooper Blackburn isn't making much of an effort to find any different suspects," I stated. Just the thought of that pompous trooper made me see red. How could Douglas remain so calm when I wanted to scratch that man's eyes out?

"C'mon, let's get this stuff sorted and packed up," Doug said as he drew up another chair.

Solar lights twinkled along the curved driveway and among the flower gardens of Oak Meadow Inn; a heady aroma of roses and honeysuckle filled the air while a gentle warm breeze ruffled my hair as we walked toward the entrance. It felt like dejá vu. Everything appeared to be the same as the night of our reunion and yet it wasn't. How could it be?

I adjusted the lightweight sweater across my bare shoulders as we entered the cooler air-conditioned inn. My sleeveless sundress looked demure yet dressy enough for dinner in an upscale restaurant, but this time I dressed for comfort in low-heeled sandals. I had to admit to myself that I wasn't cut out for high heels and fashion model clothes; I was just a housewife and mother in a small town. No need to put on airs. Tonight, I was just being myself.

"What do you think? Formal Kenyon dining room or something more casual like the Buckeye room?" Doug asked as he escorted me across the lobby.

"Casual, definitely more casual. Let's see what the Buckeye room offers."

"Good, I've got a taste for wings and pizza tonight."

"Sounds fine, but not too spicy on the wings," I cautioned.

We stopped at the doorway of the sports themed dining room, read the sign that indicated seat yourself, then paused as we searched for a secluded table in one of the back corners. I pointed to a small table for two adjacent to a wide window near the far corner. We headed toward it; a waiter followed us and laid down several napkins on the table.

"Good evening. I'm Bob, I'll be serving you tonight. What can I get you to drink?"

"I'll have a Bud Light and my wife will have a Dr. Pepper," replied Doug with a glance to me to confirm. He knows I always order the same soda.

"This is nice. I don't think I've ever eaten here before. Colleen and I peeked in to see all the OSU memorabilia when we were here decorating for the reunion Friday morning. Pretty impressive

102

collection. I think there's a program and a football both sporting Woody Hayes' autograph," I said.

The waiter brought our beverages and menus, but we only needed a quick scan to order a medium-sized pepperoni pizza and a dozen barbeque wings to share. I sipped my soda as I watched the setting sun drop lower in the sky and gray clouds clustered, foretelling a chance of rain. The window near us caught the glow of the orange sunset as the Tiffany pendant lights above each bistro table popped on, bathing the surface in a soft amber pool.

Doug reached for my hand and squeezed it lightly. He smiled at me as our eyes met in silent communication.

"I wish we could just enjoy the evening and not think about the real reason we're here," I sighed.

"No reason why we can't. I just want to replay the timeline, get the chain of events clear in my head," Doug said. "Got a pen in your purse?"

I rummaged in the bottom of my handbag until my fingers touched a ballpoint pen, then handed it to him. Doug picked up one of the paper napkins and started jotting down times and notes.

"Let's start from when we arrived, that was about six-thirty, right?"

"Yes, I think so. I had planned for us to arrive early in case any last-minute details needed attention, but I was surprised at how many other people had shown up early too. Then Colleen and I went to speak with Ricardo about the food," I stated.

Doug made a few more notes on his napkin. "Buffet was announced at eight if I recall correctly."

"Right. Ricardo was adamant about not serving the entrees before then."

"So, if Ricardo was busy in the kitchen up until then, he would not have laid his knife down before that time. Sound reasonable? If anyone picked up that knife, it would have been after that."

"I went to the ladies' room then stepped outside after we had selected our dinner plates from the buffet, probably around eight-thirty or thereafter. That's when I met Hilda and later, I heard a woman arguing behind the building," I stated as my mind replayed the scene. "Where did you get off to? When I got back to the table, you were gone."

"Guess that was when I took a minute to confront Kirkland by the kitchen doorway, but it wasn't any longer than a minute, I swear. When I entered the banquet room again, I saw the servers had cleared our table, so I went back over to the buffet to load up a new plate of food for you," Doug said.

"What are you thinking? I can see the worry in your eyes," I whispered urgently.

Doug shoved the napkin toward me to read his notes. He had underlined a glaring gap in the timeline and location; it pointed an accusing finger right at him. I knew any good investigator would question it too.

"I'm thinking I look guilty, yet I know I'm not. How do I prove it?"

"Honey, wait a minute, don't you see; I saw Hilda and maybe heard her outside. What if that was when she argued and fought with someone? She could have stabbed her assailant in self-defense before they turned the knife on her. Maybe she had picked up the knife from the kitchen. Ricardo said it was visible, lying on the prep table. Bryan was stabbed in the shoulder; Hilda could have done that."

"No, think about it Babe, that idea won't work. Bryan tried to cut in when we were dancing. Must have been around nine-forty-five by then and he wasn't bleeding from a knife wound. He had to have been stabbed after that," Doug speculated.

"Oh, you're right. Well maybe he fought with Hilda later than I thought. This is getting complicated," I said as Bob brought our food and Doug hastily slipped his notes into a pocket.

The waiter set plates and silverware in front of us then offered to serve the first slice of pizza. I nodded in agreement then reached for the tongs to place a couple of wings on both of our plates too. The food smelled and tasted delicious. We were both enjoying our pizza when a commotion and angry voices drew our attention.

Two men sat at the far end of the bar, gesturing wildly and pounding fists on the bar top to emphasize each point of their disagreement. I didn't recognize the heavy-set man, but the other was definitely Bryan Kirkland. Even from a distance across the room, I could tell he was drunk again.

"What's the problem over there?" Doug asked our server as he stopped by our table with beverage refills.

"Just a football squabble. If it gets any more heated, the bartender will toss them both out. That Kirkland dude insists Alabama's Crimson Tide will roll over the Buckeyes every time. You know we take our football seriously in here, especially OSU football. Talk like that is bound to inspire a fight among Buckeye fans," the waiter explained.

"How odd. Bryan was always a diehard Buckeye fan when we were in high school," I said. I watched the men gesticulate expansively; the heavy man almost fell off his barstool.

"Every time that dude comes in here, he tries to put down OSU. I don't know what his problem is," the waiter said disgusted.

"Wait a second, you've seen him here before? Recently?"

"Yeah, he's been in three or four times over the last month or so."

"Hmm," I mumbled. The waiter left and I absent-mindedly picked up a chicken wing as my mind processed this new information.

"What are you thinking? I see wheels turning in that pretty head of yours," Doug inquired.

"Well, Colleen and I thought Bryan had just arrived in town before the reunion. Colleen only received his RSVP the morning of the party. Now it appears he has been here a couple of months. Strange. Why hasn't anyone seen him before this? Where's he been and why's he been hiding? Don't you find that odd?"

"I dunno, maybe he's just been busy sorting out his dad's stuff or simply taking care of the property. I'm sure he's had his reasons," Doug said as he munched on a wing.

"I don't like it. The Bryan I remember would have contacted his friends as soon as he got into town. He always craved attention; I can't picture him being a loner." My fingers toyed with the miniature Brutus Buckeye on our table as my mind struggled to make sense of the situation.

"Just so long as he stays out of my path, I'm happy," Doug murmured and reached for another slice of pizza.

"Hey, you do realize that if Bryan has been here several times, then he's got to be fairly familiar with the layout of the inn," I stated, pointing my wing bone to mark my argument with each word that I spoke. "That bears thinking about."

Chapter 13

Colleen and I stood next to the rack of summer tops on sale at Frannie's Frocks. We flipped through the brightly colored tanks and tunics, moving one hangar after another as we approved or rejected the clothing. Aunt Fran receives new stock every week and always calls me so I can check out the latest merchandise when she first displays it. Today my mind wasn't on admiring the pretty tops.

"I just don't know, Colleen. What do you think?"

"About the blouse?" asked Colleen.

"No, silly, about Bryan. . . what I told you about his criticism of the Buckeyes and hiding out the last month or so," I replied.

"I admit it seems out of character for Bryan, but then again, we don't really know him anymore. After all, he's been gone over fifteen years and served in the army, even fought in a war. He's not a teenager, people do change," Colleen argued.

"Yeah, I know, but still. . . maybe we should pay him a visit," I said as my mind tried to conjure a plausible reason to barge in on him.

"Pay who a visit?" asked Aunt Fran as she moved near the display of tops. She arranged a bold floral blouse on a mannequin, added a floppy beach hat and pair of sunglasses, then surveyed her appearance. She shook her head no and removed the hat and tried another.

"I was thinking we should pay a call on the Kirkland mansion, just to be polite, check on Bryan, maybe see if his injury has healed.

What do you think?" I asked my aunt. I tried to read her expression as she faced me with arched eyebrows and her lips pressed into a firm line.

"What are you up to, Meredith? Operation ID was a success; we did our bit and learned Hilda's name. We're done now. Let the police take it from here," Aunt Fran insisted.

"Yes, but. . . I just can't stand by and wait for them to officially arrest Doug. Do you see anyone else being questioned?"

"Let me understand you. You think Bryan Kirkland may be responsible for killing that poor woman, so you want to charge into his home and do what? Accuse him? Have you considered what you will do if he is guilty? Suppose he attacks you, then what? It sounds too dangerous to me," Aunt Fran warned.

"Hmm, I'll think about it. Hey, I need an energy booster. How about a coffee and danish from Martha's?" I offered to Colleen and my aunt hoping to change the subject.

"Now I agree with you," my aunt said with a smile. She kissed me on the cheek, then gathered up her price tags and marker pen and set them on the counter next to her register. "Bring me back a dark roast coffee and one of Martha's cranberry muffins." She reached into her cash drawer for some money, but I waved her back.

"My treat. We'll be back as soon as we can," I assured her.

Colleen and I walked the block and a half distance to Martha's Bakery. The bell above the door jingled as we entered; our nostrils filled with all the delicious spices and aromas of baked breads and cakes fresh out of the oven. I'd gain twenty pounds just breathing in the tempting treats if I worked here.

Martha boxed a dozen chocolate brownies for her customer then turned to greet us. "Hi girls, what can I tempt you with today?"

"You know us all too well. Aunt Fran wants a cranberry muffin and a large cup of your dark roast coffee, but I need you to wait on that until we're ready to leave so it'll be hot. I'd like a cherry danish and a cup of coffee with cream, please."

Colleen studied the glass case, her eyes lit up when she spied a lemon meringue pie with one slice left. "I'll have that pie with a cup of tea please."

"I'll pay for everything," I told Martha as I reached for my wallet.

Martha rung up the bill then plated our desserts. We sat at one of her cute bistro tables along the front wall. The bell above the door rang again as we sipped on our drinks and savored the sinful desserts. I glanced toward the entrance and recognized Ted Williams striding into the bakery.

"Hello ladies," he beamed. His eyes sparkled and a grin stretched from ear to ear. "Martha, I'd like one of your best cheesecakes, the kind with fruit on top. I'm treating the office!"

"I've got the perfect cake," Martha said as she tucked in the corners of a cardboard box and gently set inside a chilled cheesecake spread with sugared blueberries on top.

"Hi Ted. You look like you're celebrating," I commented as I waved him over to our table.

"Actually, I am. Just signed my ultimate dream listing, the Kirkland mansion. I've had my eye on that property for years," Ted declared.

Ted Williams is well-liked around town; he manages his own real estate office as both an agent and a developer. He sold me my colonial house eleven years ago and since then he and his wife Barbara have become close friends. Their son, Joey, is a member of my cub scout den and is best buddies, practically inseparable, with my oldest son Johnny. Last year, Ted coped with being falsely accused of murder during one of our scout camping trips. Luckily, he was absolved with his reputation restored, but it was touch and go for a while.

I couldn't believe my ears. "The Kirkland mansion – up for sale? Bryan is putting the house on the market," I stated in disbelief.

"Yep, just got back with a listing agreement signed, sealed and delivered. I've got to stop back later and take photos for a big spread I want to do online and put together a sales brochure. Stupid me, I left my 35mm camera back in the office. But Kirkland was okay with my catching the shots later," Ted explained.

Thoughts spun in my head as I rapidly hatched a plan. "Would you like some help, Ted? I'm free this afternoon, I wouldn't mind lending you a hand. I was hoping to spend more time with Bryan if he's going to be home; we didn't really have a chance to catch up at the reunion," I lied and hoped my friend did not hear the insincerity in my voice.

Colleen shot me an incredulous look, her frown and arched eyebrows spoke volumes to me. I lightly kicked her foot under the table, warning her to remain silent and returned her glare before quickly pasting a wide smile on my face as Ted's attention turned from Martha back to us.

"You sure, Merry? I could use an extra pair of hands with measuring a few of the main rooms. It shouldn't take me too long to get the photographs that I want of the first floor and exterior shots," Ted said.

"Okay, great. Want me to meet you there? I may have an errand to run when we're finished," I said.

"Yeah, fine." Ted glanced at his watch before suggesting, "Can you meet me at two o'clock?"

"No problem," I said. I nodded again and smiled as Ted exited the bakery. I turned back to Colleen, expecting to hear her explode.

"What did you just do?" Colleen hissed. "I almost choked listening to you sweetly offer to assist Ted with his photography. What are you really planning?"

"This gives me the perfect excuse to get into the house. I can't believe Bryan is putting it on the market. His family has lived there over a hundred years. Earl Kirkland isn't even cold in his grave and would likely roll over if he knew the family home is being sold."

"I admit that was a shock. Now that he's back, I thought Bryan would make a life for himself in Ohio," Colleen wondered aloud.

"Maybe he needs the money. That old house and the parcel of land it sits on should fetch a pretty penny. I've got to ask Ted what the listing price is." A thousand questions and speculations popped into my mind. "Oh my goodness, wait until Aunt Fran hears the news."

We gulped down our tepid coffee and tea then swallowed the last piece of our desserts, forgotten in the hubbub. Martha prepared Aunt Fran's order. I grabbed the bag with its muffin tucked inside while Colleen held the foam cup of coffee. In an unspoken agreement, we speed walked back to the dress shop in record time.

I burst through the entrance of the store and nearly plowed into one of Meadowood's oldest citizens.

Mrs. Babcock waved her cane at me threateningly. "Watch where you're going missy. You are old enough to know better."

"Sorry Mrs. Babcock. I didn't see you there. Are you okay?" I tried to sound repentant as the spry old lady left the shop with another shake of her cane.

"Please try not to scare away one of my most loyal customers," Aunt Fran laughed. "You didn't have to rush just to get that hot coffee here, I can always nuke it in the microwave."

"You'll never believe what just happened!" I exclaimed as I set the bakery bag on the counter.

"I'll bite; what's got you in such an uproar?" asked Aunt Fran.

"We just talked with Ted Williams; Bryan Kirkland is putting the house up for sale. Can you believe it? The Kirkland mansion. . . that house must be at least a hundred years old. Wasn't it included on the historic registry just last year? Why on earth would Bryan sell the family home?"

"Hmm, that is news. I take it that Ted got the listing. What's it going for?" Aunt Fran questioned as she sipped thoughtfully on her coffee and took a bite of muffin.

I studied my aunt's face as she clearly mulled over this piece of important community gossip. I knew she'd be considering the economic impact of this news since she sat on Meadowood's Chamber of Commerce.

"Ted's taking me with him to the Kirkland place at two o'clock. I'm gonna help him with some measurements and photographs," I stated.

"Whaaat? You're determined to snoop, aren't you?"

"Don't you see? This is the perfect chance for me to get into that house, have a look around, plus I won't be alone. Ted will be there. I'll be perfectly safe, so you don't need to worry," I said.

"Uh huh, what could go wrong?" mumbled Aunt Fran and shook her head. "What about you, Colleen? Are you running off to join Miss Nancy Drew here?"

"No, I have a meeting with several of my teachers later today. Afraid Merry is on her own with this caper," Colleen answered.

"I'll be fine. You'll see; Bryan is up to something and I plan on finding out just what. I know he is mixed up with Hilda Moran somehow," I said emphatically as I waved to them both and left the store.

Kirkland Mansion presided over the village of Meadowood like an ancient castle with its serfs of medieval times. The stately stone edifice rose three stories high, with a wide veranda in the front and angled east and west wings surrounded by formal gardens. Smaller buildings, tack rooms, and horse stables with pastures now occupied only ten acres of its original three thousand acres of land claimed at the turn of the twentieth century. From its prominent position on a nearby hillside, the mansion looked down onto the town of Meadowood with its quaint shops and smaller homes. Was it any wonder that Earl Kirkland, and generations of his family before him, thought he was a king and could arrogantly reign over his neighbors?

I pulled in and parked next to Ted William's car in the wide driveway that ran along the side and to the rear of the building; my dented minivan was definitely out of place in this posh setting. I hurried to join Ted and walked around to the front entrance where he was setting up a tripod for his camera. I stood next to Ted as he snapped multiple shots of the exterior of the house. I had to admire the neoclassical architecture of the mansion; four tall doric columns supported the veranda and upper story, their narrow flutes ended in an elaborate frieze. Gracefully carved cornices topped each long window frame filled with symmetrical nine over nine panes of glass.

As we walked toward the wide front portal, I inspected the building more closely and noticed the flecks of paint peeling from window frames, the tarnished brass doorknobs, broken pieces of slate in the vestibule, all signs that the mansion had fallen into disrepair. We stepped into a dark shadowy foyer and paused to get our bearings.

"Let me open these draperies," Ted said as he went to draw back the heavy brocade fabric from four windows. Warm afternoon sunlight instantly poured into the space, brightening the gloomy room.

"Oh, much better. Place looks like a funeral home. How can Bryan stand to live here?" I asked and shivered despite the warmth of the summer day. The black velvet upholstery on heavy settees and other dark furnishings added to the oppressive atmosphere in the room. Mahogany hardwood floors, dull with age and poor care, stretched the length of the foyer and center hall. The floor plan arranged rooms on each side of the entry, all closed off with heavy wooden doors.

"I know what you mean. I have my work cut out for me to stage this place and make it more cheerful before considering an open house. It'll never show well like this," Ted said as he opened more draperies.

"Okay, so where do you want to start? Is Bryan here, by the way?"

"No, Bryan told me he'd be out. Let's start in the drawing room then move into the library. I need dimensions of each room."

"Where are all the servants? The one time I was here, back when Bryan and I dated in high school, there must have been at least a dozen servants. Now I don't see anyone," I said.

"I know, it's a shame. Kirkland used to be a major employer around here: a butler, maids, cooks, gardeners and stable lads. This place was a regular Downton Abbey, now I think there's just one cleaning lady who comes in once a week.

You know, I recall my granddad telling me when I was a kid about the wonderful Christmas parties he attended here. Must have been back when my granddad was a young man during the roaring twenties; the Kirkland family included the town's folk in their annual holiday celebrations back then and was quite the benefactor to Meadowood. Guess things changed after the big stock market crash; Kirkland lost investments like everyone else," Ted explained as he moved about the room making notes. He stretched out his measuring tape as I held the other end and walked to the far wall.

We moved into the library. "Oh phew, this place is so musty! Can we open a window?" I complained while coughing in the stale air.

Floor to ceiling walnut bookcases lined two walls of the library. Faded leather book bindings graced volumes of the classics; my fingers traced various titles written by Charles Dickens, Henry David Thoreau, Ralph Waldo Emerson, and Alexander Dumas. I scanned the shelves, admiring the numerous American histories, biographies and science books. The far wall held a set of doors covered in sheer curtains, now yellowed and fragile. A pair of Queen Anne chairs flanked a round Chippendale reading table and a deep burgundy, leather sofa was positioned opposite a wide fireplace hearth. A large portrait, painted in oils, of a brooding Kirkland ancestor hung above the mantle. A thin layer of dust covered the thick Aubusson carpeting.

"Sorry. Earl had become such a recluse after Madeline died and Bryan left home. Most of the house stayed closed up and I guess this room wasn't used much. It does smell a bit." Ted unlocked the pair of French doors that led to an outside patio; the doors stubbornly refused to budge but he pulled hard and managed to crack one open a few inches.

"Wow, impressive library. I never knew much about the Kirkland family history. How'd they make their money, do you know?" I asked as we measured one of the book-lined library walls.

"Steel. The first Earl Kirkland developed some kind of process for smelting pig iron; he was no Andrew Carnegie, but he did patent his process and sold it. Made a pot of money and then invested it. That's about as much as I know. Like I said, my granddad had more doings with the family than any of us."

"Well Bryan's father was as stingy as they come. I recall Bryan used to call him the original Mister Scrooge. Bryan received a small allowance when we were in high school and many times, I was the one who paid for movie tickets; it was terribly embarrassing for him. No wonder he was eager to leave home."

"From what I've been able to learn while I was researching the title records at the courthouse, the Kirkland family sold off most of their acreage to the state in 1933 following the crash. I suppose selling land was their only option for staying solvent and keeping the mansion. I imagine after falling on hard times like that, the purse strings tightened, and attitudes changed," Ted said.

"Pity the family allowed this house to get run down. A new owner could restore it to its former glory with just a little work and money," Ted speculated as he surveyed the first-floor rooms. He wandered into the dining hall and kitchen area, giving me the opportunity I had waited for.

I immediately opened the tall Chippendale secretary desk that I had spied against one of the library walls. I pulled down the writing lid to expose numerous cubby holes and tiny drawers. As quietly as I could, I slid each drawer open, peeked at the contents and poked into the cubby holes, looking for any kind of information that might explain where Bryan's been living or his motive for selling the mansion. Trying to search as quickly as I dared before Ted returned to the room, I jiggled a stuck, narrow drawer. I yanked hard and the wood budged a fraction. Picking up a slim letter opener, I slid the blade along the side of the drawer and pulled again. Success! I rummaged through a small group of receipts in the drawer, then found the object that had caused the wedge problem – a photograph. I carefully pulled it free and stared in surprise at the missing prom picture from the reunion poster. Why did Bryan take that photograph showing him and me at our junior prom? Sentimental reasons? Didn't seem likely. So why take that picture and hide it? I slipped it into my pocket to study later. I'll have to take the risk that Bryan won't find it missing from the desk.

I searched through the rest of the desk drawers but found nothing else that I thought was significant. Naturally, any legal documents would be in a safe deposit box at the bank or maybe a locked safe somewhere in the house. I didn't really expect to stumble over a copy of Earl Kirkland's will, but it sure would be interesting to read its contents. Maybe Ted will know more about that.

Framed photographs rested on the dusty fireplace mantle. I moved to study each of them; one appeared to be a family portrait of what I assumed was a youthful Earl Kirkland and his wife Madeline holding a baby that had to be Bryan. Another more recent frame held a picture of Bryan in uniform; odd, I didn't think his father had approved of Bryan joining the army. It surprised me to see the photo displayed. I picked it up to examine it closer. The back of the frame felt loose. Of course, my curiosity insisted I peek behind the backing to see what else it held. A creased piece of paper clung to the back of the photograph. I unfolded and read a letter of condolence from some commanding officer with regrets on the death of his son. What? How can that be? I stared at the printed paper in the palm of my hand. This letter had to be a terrible mistake; clearly Bryan was alive and well.

I folded the yellow slip of paper and stuffed it into my pocket to join the confiscated photograph. I gently attached the back of the frame again and returned the photo to its place on the mantle, minus the keepsake telegram. Hearing Ted approach the library door, I rushed back to the secretary desk and hurried to close the desk lid.

Satisfied that I returned all to normal, I smiled at my friend as he entered the library and we prepared to leave.

Ted carefully locked the front door and we walked to our parked cars just as Bryan arrived home. Recognizing me, he did a double take as he drove toward the garage; his face registered the shock of seeing me at his house. His look was priceless, but I didn't plan to give him any time for questioning why I was there. I jumped into my minivan and sped away with the discovered treasures tucked safely into my pocket.

Chapter 14

Questions rolled and tumbled across my mind like dice cubes in a Yahtzee game as I drove toward town. Should I go home and share my findings with Doug or seek advice from Aunt Fran and the girls? Maybe I should wait to show Doug until I have more evidence, then present the case. My minivan, like a trusted steed, made the decision for me as I unconsciously found myself stopping in front of Frannie's Frocks. I sat behind the wheel, lost in thought and stared ahead, unseeing. Brisk tapping on the car window made me jump guiltily; my heart rose in my throat.

"You coming in?" asked Aunt Fran, her brow wrinkled with a concerned frown.

"You scared me half to death! Don't sneak up on someone like that," I shrieked.

"What planet were you on?" Aunt Fran laughed as she pulled open my car door.

I trudged behind her into the vacant store; no customers lingered over racks of swimsuits or summer frocks. Where are all the shoppers that normally pop in to browse during a pleasant afternoon? I glanced at the clock on the far wall and was dismayed to see how late it had become. Working with Ted at the Kirkland Mansion took longer than I had realized. Now I really felt guilty for staying away from home so long and leaving Doug alone. I could arrange my timetable and personal routine far easier when my husband was in his office during the day.

"Good gracious gal, you look like you lost your best friend. So, what happened at the Kirkland place? Did you get to snoop or just play assistant to Ted?"

"Can I get something cold to drink, Aunt Fran? Any of that iced tea left in the fridge? I'll tell you all about it, but right now I'm so thirsty, I'm gonna die. I had no idea how long we were taking to do those measurements; Doug will have a fit. Holy cow, you should see the inside of that place; right out of a gothic novel."

My aunt placed the closed sign on the front door and locked it then strode into her rear break room to retrieve a tall ice-filled glass of tea. She handed me the tumbler and waited while I took a healthy swallow to quench my parched throat.

"Okay, now spill. What happened," she demanded.

"Mmm, so much better. Thanks. Oh my gosh, I don't know where to begin," I said as I plopped onto a folding chair. "Ted took lots of pictures outside with the front of the house and grounds, then we went inside. Bryan was conveniently gone, so that was a relief. The house is archaic, gloomy and smells stale. Heavy draperies cover all the windows; Ted pulled them all back so we could get some sunlight."

"Doesn't sound like a photo spread to appear in *House Beautiful*," Aunt Fran commented sarcastically.

I snorted and took another swallow of iced tea. "Ted finally left me alone when he went off to see the kitchen. I figured the library was the best place to search, so I went straight to the secretary desk and poked around in all the tiny cubby holes and drawers. I did find this," I said as I pulled out the creased photograph from my pocket.

Aunt Fran examined the picture, turned it over and read the description scribbled on the back. "Your prom picture. . . maybe Bryan's mother saved it. I don't see the significance."

"This is the same copy that was pinned onto Martha's memory board at the reunion. See the tiny thumb tack holes in the corners? Colleen and I noticed it missing on Saturday morning when we were cleaning up. Bryan must have taken it during the party. Why would he do that?"

"Maybe he just wanted a keepsake. Doesn't look very sinister to me," said Aunt Fran. She studied the picture again; a sliver of a smile came to her lips as she glanced up at me then back again to the photo. "You were so young, cute as a button."

"Humph. That's not all; wait until I show you what else I found," I said as I carefully retrieved the creased paper from my pants pocket. Slowly unfolding the yellow paper, I handed the condolence letter to my aunt.

A frown creased her forehead as eyebrows raised; her face registered surprise as she read the brief message. Aunt Fran turned the paper over and then back again as she scrutinized the paper stock, the ink, and the sender's address.

"It looks genuine, but I don't understand how that can be," Aunt Fran murmured. "Poor Earl. . . what he must have suffered

124

when he received this. No wonder the man had a heart attack. He never got to learn that Bryan was alive. So tragic."

"Seems odd that Mr. Kirkland didn't post an obituary for Bryan. Why would he keep notice of Bryan's death a secret from everyone in town? Maybe he didn't believe it. I found this tucked behind a framed photograph of Bryan in his Army dress uniform. Do you think Mr. Kirkland put it there?" I asked.

"Earl must have. Almost like a scrapbook memento, the document and photograph together."

"Wouldn't the Army confirm the identification of someone before sending out this kind of notification? How could they make such a mistake?" The negligence seemed unbelievable.

I finished my drink then scooped up my finds, tucking them back into my pocket. I rose to leave and gave my aunt a brief hug.

"What are you going to do now? Will you show these to Doug and tell him how you found them? I don't like the idea of you snooping on your own; it's not safe."

"I know, I know. I need to confess what I've been doing; Doug won't like it. Sometimes he treats me like a child; I know a lecture will be forthcoming when I show him this," I mumbled. "Better get home and prepare dinner before I get into more hot water."

A cool evening breeze tickled my face and neck as I stretched out on the chaise lounge. I breathed in the scent of the tiny white petals of the sweet alyssum plants bordering the deck. The lilac tree that Doug pampers and prunes so carefully each year awarded us with delightful blooms and fragrance this summer. Our flower garden looked so pretty and smelled delightful too, very calming.

Doug and I had retreated to our rear deck after dinner to enjoy the fading sunset plus the peace and quiet. It was a rare occasion when we could sip a glass of wine and bask in solitude without the shouts and giggles of two little boys dashing about the yard. However, my sham serenity was misleading; inside I was quaking in apprehension, deciding how I would approach Doug with the confirmation that I was indeed investigating where he had told me not to. It was a feeling I was becoming all too familiar with, rather like being sent to the principal's office when you were a kid.

"I spent part of the afternoon today helping Ted Williams," I began.

"Oh yeah? Doing what?" a distracted Doug asked, his interest still engrossed in the evening newspaper.

"Ted got the listing to sell the Kirkland Mansion; he needed help with the room measurements." Now I had his attention as he sat up straighter and tossed the paper aside.

"Oh really? Was lover boy there to ogle my wife at will?"

"Bryan was not at home, and he's certainly not my lover boy. Will you just put away that green monster and listen to me? I have something important to show you," I pleaded. I reached for him but dropped my hand in frustration as he turned away. My jaw tightened;

I made a conscious effort not to grind the enamel off my teeth. Sometimes we were on completely different wavelengths.

"Sorry. What is it? You said it's important." Doug shifted in his seat, dragged his fingers through his hair impatiently then waited for me to continue my tale. I could see him trying to control his emotions as much as me.

"I found a couple of things while I was in the Kirkland library, a photograph and a telegram. I don't understand it; it just doesn't feel right. Look at these," I said as I handed the yellowed paper and worn photograph to my husband.

Doug turned the items over and over as he studied the prom picture and read the telegram notice. He glanced at me, then pointed at the picture he instantly recognized.

"Isn't this the same one I saw on that poster? See the pin holes in the corners? Think Kirkland took it because you're in it with him or he just wanted to annoy us? I'm wondering if maybe there's another reason." He studied the picture again as he rubbed his whiskered jaw.

"If he only wanted to annoy me or you, why hide the photograph? I found it crammed into a hidden desk drawer. What do you think of the condolence letter? Why would the Army be so negligent and not verify someone's death before sending out such a terrible message?" I asked, my indignation rising as I thought of the tragic consequences it had caused.

"I can tell you from my experience serving in the Army; when it comes to a fallen soldier, the Army does not make mistakes. I've

127

seen bodies blown up or so badly burnt, their own mothers would not know them, but the Army always runs a DNA test and fingerprints to determine an identity."

"I understand what you're saying, but how does that explain why poor Earl Kirkland got a notice of his son's death when clearly he's not?" My mind puzzled over the confusing facts of the situation.

"There is another solution to the puzzle. . . Bryan Kirkland could be an imposter," Doug said thoughtfully as he read the telegram again, noted the date, then sat back in his chair to mull over this alternative possibility.

"Oh my gosh, I don't see how. I mean, just look at him in this photograph and compare it to him in the flesh — it's the same man. Surely. . . wait a minute, Big Jim said Hilda was mooning over a boyfriend who had died, and she wanted to see where he used to live, that's why she traveled cross-country. What if Hilda kept a picture or some love letters? If she loved this guy, she's bound to have kept everything he ever gave her. I know I would."

"Strong possibility, but her possessions are probably being held by the state investigation team by now," Doug said.

"Can you call Tony and ask? Humph, they didn't even know her name until I told you; maybe they don't know where she was living either. But I do," I grinned wickedly. "Give Tony a quick call. Let's pay a visit to Hilda's motel room," I whispered excitedly.

"Are you crazy? Do you want me to lose my job? Bad enough I'm on suspension."

"Oh c'mon, you went snooping around with Tony at the Inn. But I understand, you're worried about your job and all. I could just go alone or maybe I'll call Aunt Fran. She'd be up for it," I teased.

"You know damn well I am not about to let you go off half-cocked on your own in the middle of the night. I don't know how I get roped into your shenanigans; I should know better. You're a bad influence, Meredith! Wait right here while I try to reach Tony at home. He's gonna wonder why I'm asking about that gal's stuff," grumbled Doug as he walked back into the house.

I sipped my wine and smiled to myself. I'd much rather have Doug with me than Aunt Fran for breaking into a strange motel; I'm not *that* brave. There has to be a reason why Hilda came to Meadowood and why she was killed. Was Bryan pretending to be dead? Did Hilda know too much? Did Bryan kill her to silence her? Hilda told Big Jim she was coming into money, but from where or whom? If we could just find an answer to one of those questions, I was certain we'd find her murderer.

Doug came out of the house dressed in dark pants and a black pull-over shirt. He carried a flashlight and a small tool kit. His mouth drew into a line of grim determination as he approached me.

"Tony says the state guys haven't been able to locate Hilda's residence yet. They're supposed to follow up with her employer tomorrow. Naturally he asked me why I wanted to know; I had to make up some story about you giving the girl a scarf when you met her at the Inn. I doubt he bought it; but he respects me enough not to question my motives. Go change your clothes if we're gonna do this."

I jumped up then ran into the house and raced upstairs. I tossed clothes out of my closet until I found an outfit matching Doug's and for good measure, changed from my white tennis shoes to a pair of navy-blue canvas boat shoes. I giggled as I looked at my image in the mirror – ninja warrior here I come.

"Where we going?" asked Doug as I retrieved a spare flashlight from the kitchen drawer. We left one light on in the kitchen, made sure Mittens was in the house before we locked the doors, then silently hopped into the car.

"Small motel near the diner, allows extended stays. Out on Timber Trail, off state route 20, that's where she was staying, according to Margie," I explained as we headed out of town.

"Let's hope we can find the place. We don't even know which room was hers. This better be worth it," Doug grumbled.

Chapter 15

A solitary security light illuminated the sign and front of Hank's Erie Caboose Diner as we cautiously pulled into the shadowy parking lot. Doug turned in his seat toward me.

"So, this is where she worked. Okay, which way is the motel from here? You said down the road. Do we go left or right?"

"Um, I'm not sure. If we go left that's closer to Pottstown and the state highway, right?" I pondered.

"Yeah, and the other direction is just more farmland."

"So maybe we should turn left; that makes more sense for a motel to be closer to a highway. Yeah, let's go left," I said with conviction.

Gravel crunched under our tires as we pulled out of the diner's lot and headed down the road. Clouds filled the night sky obscuring any dim moonlight, perfect weather for a clandestine operation. A lone car sped past us on the desolate road. Doug proceeded slowly, glancing in the rear-view mirror every few minutes, we scanned the surrounding roadside. I grabbed Doug's arm and pointed to a short building just ahead on the right. A dim light glowed yellow in the inky night. We rolled to a stop in the shadows along the berm of the road and peered at our destination.

A single clapboard building, a faded sign painted across the entrance, designated the structure as the office. A metal placard perched precariously on a tall rusty post; yet a weary traveler could still read letters worn smooth over the years: Timber Trail Motor

Court. A gravel parking lot sat adjacent to the office and to the rear, a squat, long rectangular building with five doors comprised the sleeping quarters. A square window and door frame outlined each unit in the row; no lights shone behind the covered windows. Three cars parked in front of the row of rooms.

Doug inched the car off the berm into a grassy space, then cut the engine. The night became even darker without the beam of our headlights. We soundlessly closed car doors, stood for a moment to acclimate our eyes to the black then crept forward. I clutched my unlit flashlight in one hand and Doug's hand in the other.

Doug led me along the far side of the motel building. We kept to the shadows and onto the perimeter of soft dirt, off the gravel that crunched under our footsteps and echoed in the still night. Doug motioned to me, pointing to the two center units without vehicles as most likely to be vacant. It was as good a plan as any. He handed me a pair of rubber gloves, the kind they used at the station. We both needed to guard against leaving our prints.

I waited by the corner of the building as Doug sneaked past the end unit and the drapery covered window. He tiptoed to the next room; its window appeared uncovered, but the room was pitch black. No car was parked in front of the door marked number four. Doug pressed his face against the window and tried to peer inside. He moved to the room next door, number three, also missing a vehicle. Someone had partially drawn the draperies, leaving a narrow open space between. Again, Doug pressed his face against the pane and squinted into the dark room.

I stood listening in the silent night, unable to see anything, I almost screamed when Doug suddenly appeared out of the dark void next to my side then clamped a hand over my mouth to stifle the sound. I nodded okay and he removed his hand. He gripped my wrist and pulled me around the rear of the building. I didn't think it could get any darker, but I was wrong. I could barely see his face in the pitch blackness.

Doug whispered in my ear, "Two of the rooms are vacant but one appears recently occupied; I saw clothing laying across the bed. The other room seems to be empty; I couldn't even make out the shape of furniture in the dark."

"Can we get in?" My voice sounded loud to my ears and I cringed, praying no one heard.

Doug turned on his flashlight and kept it pointing toward the ground as we moved closer to the back wall of the building. Small square windows mounted in wooden frames could only mean bathrooms. We counted down the row and stopped under room three. Doug slipped a screwdriver out of his pocket and pried along the wooden frame. The brittle wood gave way easily as Doug pressed then raised the windowpane. He stuck his head into the opening, looked around with his flashlight then withdrew. Pulling me down with him, we crouched on the ground below the window, sitting on our haunches.

"It's the bathroom all right and the toilet is directly below the window. I'm going to lift you up then you crawl in. You can step on the toilet seat and hop down. For God's sake, don't fall or make any

133

noise. Can you do that?" he asked. I felt him studying my face in the black night.

"Are you sure I'll fit through that tiny opening? I'm not as slim as I once was, you know. But I'm game. What'll I do once I'm inside?"

"Unlock the door and I'll slip inside. Let's hope the manager doesn't live on site; but from the looks of this place, it's doubtful. Okay, you ready?"

I nodded then laid my flashlight down on the ground so both hands would be free. Doug laced his fingers together, and I placed my foot into his step as he boosted me up. I grabbed hold of the windowsill, pushed my head and shoulders through the narrow opening, then rested my belly on the frame. I wiggled forward, tumbled the rest of the way into the room and caught myself before cracking my head on the porcelain toilet tank. Not the most graceful move I've ever made.

"You okay?" Doug whispered loudly as he thrust his head through the window. "Here," he said as he waved the flashlight toward me and I grabbed it from his hand. "Count to ten, then be ready to open the door."

The flashlight beam made halos on the floor as I pointed it downward to help me see where I was walking and hopefully to prevent any light from being seen outside. I mentally counted to ten then turned off my torch before cracking the door open a few inches. Doug slipped into the room and quickly shut the portal. He moved

134

to the window and silently pulled the tattered fabric across the window. When he finished, he turned his flashlight on.

"Let's be quick about this. I can't believe I just committed breaking and entering, and I'm a cop. You search the dresser. I'll look around for any evidence that proves this is actually Hilda's room."

We kept our lights pointed low and silently moved about the room. A woman had definitely stayed here if the clothing was any proof. I slid open the top drawer of the flimsy dresser and lifted folded panties and bras. Nothing there of importance. The middle drawer contained three folded tops and a pair of jeans. She was no clothes horse, not exactly a vast wardrobe here. The bottom drawer contained a white sweater and what appeared to be a pillowcase filled with various papers and envelopes. Feeling certain that this was what we were looking for, I grabbed the cloth bag triumphantly.

Doug held a prescription bottle in his hand that he found in the bathroom. He rattled the bottle and held it out for me to read the name, Hilda Moran, on the label. No doubt about it, this had been her room.

"Look what I found. Can we take it home? There's a bunch of stuff in here," I said as I touched envelopes and scraps of paper. Reaching into the bottom of the case, my fingers skidded across a smooth texture that could only be the surface of a photograph. I pulled it out and shone my flashlight onto the glossy picture. "Oh my, look at this," I exclaimed.

Doug reached for the picture and held his own light onto the figures in the frame, a woman stood between two men. The woman was definitely Hilda. "Keep this. We can't take the entire contents of that pillowcase. How would we explain it? I don't know how we'll explain the picture, for that matter, but we can't take the whole thing."

"Maybe one or two letters?" I asked as I dipped into the pillowcase and latched onto several envelopes containing letters. I studied the fronts of the envelopes under my flashlight, tossed back one that was only a credit card statement, and grinned at two that were handwritten letters sent from a military APO address. I tucked them into my pocket. No one will miss two little letters from this big stack.

"Let's get out of here. I don't feel lucky," Doug said as he carefully returned the medicine bottle to the bathroom cabinet.

I stuffed the pillowcase back into the bottom dresser drawer and pressed it flat so the drawer could slide shut. I quickly glanced about the room, didn't appear we moved anything out of place. At least I hoped not. I turned toward a small sound and groped my way in the dark to find Doug closing the bathroom window and locking it to hold the frame in place.

"How are we getting out of here if you've got the window closed?"

"Extremely carefully through that front door. You don't think I was going to squeeze through that window, did you? Then how would we close it? Stay low and quiet when you get outside and head back into the brush on the left," Doug instructed.

We moved back toward the door, switched off our lights, turned the lock on the motel room's door handle then cracked the door open just wide enough to slip out. I ran blindly toward the edge of the property and prayed I wouldn't trip and fall in the dark. I stumbled once but felt my husband grab my arm to steady me as we ran toward our car. Relief poured over me as I slid into my seat and Doug started the engine. We drove away with headlights off until we were well clear of the motel and could safely turn them on.

The clock on the dashboard glowed midnight. . . the bewitching hour. In our haste to get away, we didn't spot the other vehicle waiting and watching ominously in the dark.

Too keyed up to sleep, I studied the pages of the letter arranged on the table before me. I sipped a cup of herbal tea, hoping it would soothe my frayed nerves, and read again the return address on the envelope, no name, just a P.O. Box with an Army unit number and an overseas APO zip code. Typical military address used by every serviceman. However, the letter read more interesting. Definitely a romantic message sent from a soldier to the girl he left behind. He talked about the hardships and loneliness of being away from home and how much he missed her. Water drops smudged the date on the letter (2/3/2011), but if I was interpreting it correctly, it read February or maybe it was March. I never was any good at reading those military date formats with the day before the month instead of stating the month name first then the day like the rest of the world. Guess it didn't matter, one month or the other. I was caught up in the emotion expressed within the letter. I skimmed through to the last page and searched for a signature – *"Buddy"*. Who was Buddy?

I don't know what I was expecting. Did I really think I'd see Bryan Kirkland's signature with love and kisses? To say I was disappointed would be an understatement.

I reached for the second letter that I had confiscated from the collection. This one was clearly dated in December, since he started his greeting with merry Christmas wishes. Rubbing my eyes, as sleep overtook me, I tried to focus on the words in the letter. The writer seemed to answer questions from one of Hilda's previous letters but the tone of his words seemed clipped, almost angry. I started to fold the pages and put them away when a phrase jumped off the page. I stopped and smoothed out the page to read again his promise to her that he would make amends with his father and heal the wound that had kept them separated for so many years.

"Hey, you coming to bed?" called Doug from upstairs. "Look at that stuff in the morning; it'll be here soon enough."

"You're right. I'm so tired, I can't keep my eyes open.

Scooping up the letters and envelopes, I laid them on my desk, added the photographs and telegram to them and covered the pile with a heavy cookbook to hold them in place.

"Come on Mittens, let's hit the sack," I said as I turned off the kitchen light and dragged my feet up the stairs.

Chapter 16

Colleen knocked three times on our kitchen door before my muddled mind registered what the noise was. I managed to shuffle toward the door, remove the lock, and wave her in as I stumbled back toward the coffee pot. Caffeine, I definitely needed a transfusion of caffeine to wake me this morning. I swear, I will never stay up that late again; five hours of sleep is not enough.

"What happened to you?" Colleen asked with a laugh. "You look worse than what the cat dragged in."

"Didn't get to bed until late; my body is punishing me this morning. What time is it anyway? What are you doing here, by the way?" I asked in between great gulps of hot coffee. My droopy eyelids finally lifted open.

"Don't you remember? We have to stop by Oak Meadow and settle up with their final invoice. We have a balance due for the reunion's extra food they served. I think it's pretty nice of their management to give us time to settle our own accounts and wait on their payment, not every place would do that," Colleen said as she poured herself a mug of coffee and stirred in a splash of milk.

"Mm-hmm, I'll be awake soon. Just give me some time to throw on some clothes and wash the sleep from my face. Oh my gosh, I feel like someone drugged me. Now I know what those articles mean when they talk about sleep deprivation. I haven't felt this drained since the boys were babies with three o'clock feedings," I groaned.

Colleen laughed again and patted me on the back. "Tell Doug no more all-night love making sessions if this is what it does to you in the morning!"

"What?" I started to ask, confused, then realized the reason Colleen attributed to my sleeplessness. Going along with her misconception, I smiled at her and made a face, "Ha ha, wouldn't you like to know."

"Where is the man of the house, anyway?" Colleen asked.

"I have no idea. He got up and out before I woke."

"Well, shake a leg, sleepy head, we've got things to do and people to see," said Colleen and made a shooing motion with her hands, pushing me toward the stairs.

Mittens meowed and stood by his empty bowl. He shot me a disapproving look. I was clearly falling down on my duties.

"Rowwr," Mittens circled his dish again.

"Go on up, I'll take care of feeding the cat. Go ahead," Colleen stated as she opened and closed cupboard doors until she located Mitten's bag of dry cat food. She poured a generous amount into his bowl and then treated him with a fresh dish of milk.

"There you go big fella, that ought to hold you," she said as she gave him a scratch behind his ears and was duly rewarded with loud purring.

It took the force of the shower spray hitting my face to chase the sleep away. I shampooed my hair quickly, toweled it dry and added a touch of mousse to fluff my curls. No time for any makeup today. I

140

quickly donned a pair of black and white gingham capris and a black sleeveless tunic. Slipping on a pair of white sandals, I ran downstairs to join Colleen.

"Sorry. Did I keep you waiting long?" I asked.

"No problem; you could qualify for a quick-change artist, that was barely fifteen minutes. I wish I could get ready in the morning for school that fast."

"Thanks, but you learn to make every second count when you have little kids clamoring for your attention. Time in the bathroom becomes a luxury, believe me. Okay, so let's get going. Do you have the invoice?"

"Yes. Do you have the checkbook for the reunion account?" Colleen asked.

"Oh dear, good thing you said something. It's in my desk drawer. Just a second," I said as I pulled open my file and retrieved the check register. My eyes fell on the pictures and letters poking out from under the large cookbook on my desktop where I had dropped them the night before. On impulse, I grabbed the picture stolen from Hilda's room and stuffed it into my purse along with the checkbook.

"Wait until I show you what I found yesterday," I told Colleen as I slid into the passenger seat of her Ford Mustang. I sighed, remembering how fun it used to be to drive a sports car and for a moment I envied my single friend. But images of my two adorable sons flashed in my mine and I knew I'd be happy to drive a beat-up minivan for the rest of my life.

"Isn't it a gorgeous day?" Colleen asked as we sped out of town with the convertible top down and the wind blowing our hair. Colleen's long hair whipped behind her like an auburn pennant waving in the bright blue sky.

"Almost makes me forget the horror of the past few days," I agreed. Almost, but not quite. There was still a murder to solve and the need to clear my husband's name.

In all too short a time, we arrived at the Oak Meadow Inn and parked the car in the visitor's space. Colleen and I strolled into the lobby and turned toward the administrative offices located down a short hallway in the east wing. Housekeeping staff vacuumed and dusted the main floor and public rooms; reservation clerks were busy behind the front reception area. Everyone bustled about in a quick tempo today except me.

Colleen knocked lightly on the manager's door. We waited in the hall for Gary Bates to acknowledge us. I could hear him through the closed office door speaking with someone and assumed he was on the phone.

"Hope he finishes his call soon," I said, tapping my foot, my sleepless night making me impatient.

"I usually don't mind waiting, though it is rather annoying since I made an appointment with him to take care of this bill," Colleen said.

"Let's go comb our hair. Mine looks like a rat's nest now."

"Okay, he can wait on us for a change," agreed Colleen.

We hurried back to the lobby and sought the restrooms I recalled near the entrance to the Buckeye Room. As I turned to push open the ladies' room door, I thought I saw Bryan Kirkland out of the corner of my eye. I swung around to get a better look, but the aisle was empty.

"You go ahead; I think I just spotted Bryan. Wonder what he's doing here? I'll just be a second; meet you back at Gary's office," I told Colleen as I left to search for Bryan. I wandered through wings of the inn and peeked into open rooms and behind doors. I poked my head into the Kenyon dining room, saw no one, and continued toward the banquet hall. Empty. *"Maybe it wasn't him; just my imagination,"* I thought.

I started back toward the manager's office when suddenly I felt a hand on my back propelling me toward a narrow door. My feet slid along the tiled floor. Cold metal pressed against my neck. Is that a knife?!

"Hey! Stop it," I yelled and tried to twist away.

Seconds later, someone forcefully pushed and thrust into a dark closet. Hands tried to rip my purse from my grasp; I instinctively fought to hold on to the shoulder strap of the bag and pulled with all my might to prevent its theft.

A muffled voice growled a warning, "Back off!"

I screamed at the top of my lungs, "Help, help!"

My assailant let go of the bag so suddenly that the momentum threw me off balance and I stumbled against the contents of the cramped confine. I heard a click. Righting myself, I scrambled blindly to find the doorknob. I jiggled the handle to confirm it was locked. I pounded on the solid wood door and twisted the handle again.

"Somebody let me out," I shouted. I could hear footsteps but could not judge their nearness. I called out again, "Help, let me out."

Moments later, a very stunned house maid yanked the door open. Her hand flew to her mouth as she gaped at me crushed between mops and brooms.

"Are you all right, madam? How did you get locked into the closet?" the maid inquired.

"I think I'm okay. Thank you for coming to my rescue."

Someone took a big risk to try and steal a handbag. What could he have been after? As soon as I asked myself the question, the answer popped into my mind – the photograph from Hilda's room. How could anyone know I had that?

I glanced about to see several people in the corridor; were they investigating the source of the disturbance or perhaps one was the cause? I spotted Ricardo standing at the far end of the hall near the kitchen entrance; Gary Bates stood in his doorway; I recognized our waiter Bob, from the other night, watching me from the Buckeye Room. Could any of them be capable of locking me into a closet? Would one of them threaten me?

Colleen rushed toward me; concern written all over her face.

"Oh my God, what happened?" Colleen clutched me in a protective hug then released me slowly; her eyes searched my face for answers.

"I'll tell you later. Right now I don't trust anyone. Let's get this bill paid and get out of here," I said as I walked toward the manager's office with checkbook in hand.

Chapter 17

We drove back to town in a somber mood, no longer feeling carefree with the breeze in our hair. Colleen had even put up the top on the Mustang and we locked all our doors as soon as we climbed into the car. No place felt safe or secure any more.

"Let's go to my aunt's house. I have a photo I want to show to both of you and need your opinions. She's home today; it's her day off. Betty Jones runs the shop on Wednesdays."

Colleen drove to the small cottage on Elm Street and parked out front. My aunt's SUV was parked in the drive, evidence that she was home. I knocked lightly on the front door then opened it as I called out.

"Aunt Fran, it's Merry and Colleen."

"C'mon in. What brings you gals by?" answered my aunt from the kitchen doorway.

I always felt a sense of calm and security wash over me when I entered my aunt's cozy cottage with its serene turquoise and soft chocolate brown decor. Several water-color seascapes adorned cream-colored walls; studying the art always left me with a sense of ocean waves rushing to the shore and warm sand tickling your toes. Her home begged you to stay awhile and cuddle up. However, today my nerves were in such a jangle that even being here did not help.

"What's happened? You're both as white as a ghost," Aunt Fran stated as she took one look at our stricken faces.

"Merry's been assaulted," declared Colleen as she plopped down onto the chocolate suede sofa.

"What? Oh my God! Are you all right; did you call the police? Where's Doug?" Aunt Fran fired off questions as she paced the floor.

I collapsed onto a plush recliner and cried. Suddenly, I couldn't stop the tears streaming down my cheeks.

"Assault. . . what does that mean exactly? Sexual assault? She's in shock. Merry needs to go to the hospital immediately," Aunt Fran stated as she rushed to my side and enveloped me in her arms.

"Oh no, I'm sorry; I didn't mean that kind of assault. Goodness! No, we were at the Oak Meadow Inn when someone attacked Merry with a knife at her throat and locked her in a closet. She wasn't hurt, but it scared us both," Collen explained, still shaken from the event.

I sniffed and sniveled, trying to get my water works under control. I reached for a tissue and blew my nose loudly then looked sheepishly between my friend and aunt. "Sorry. I don't know what came over me."

"It's all right, you go ahead and cry. However, you didn't answer me; did you call the police?" Aunt Fran asked.

"Well, no. I have no idea who did it and I wasn't hurt. I'm sure it was only a prank, shoving me into a closet," I explained, sniffling and wiping my nose again.

"Uh huh, a prank does not have someone hold a knife to your throat. I don't like the sound of this one bit, Meredith. It was one thing to try and identify that woman, bit of a lark, and I got a kick out of my role in it, but now. . . You've gone and become involved in this

147

murder and it's become treacherous, just like I warned you it would," Aunt Fran lectured me angrily. She took a seat across from me, studying the pair of us as she tried to quiet her own fears.

"I'm sorry, Aunt Fran." I winced at her verbal chastisement. I know my aunt meant well; she was just concerned, but I had to defend my actions. "I never meant to get so involved, but I just cannot idly stand by while my husband is being accused of a crime that I know he didn't commit. I have to help him."

"Meredith always runs off half-crazy, but you," she wagged her finger at Colleen, "I thought you would know better, and a school principal too. What were you both doing at Oak Meadow?"

Colleen sat up straighter and justified our actions. "Honestly, we were there on business. Meredith is treasurer and I'm the head of the reunion committee. We had an appointment with the manager to settle our bill for the reunion party; we owed money for the extra food they catered. That's the only reason we went, just to pay the final invoice."

"Well, that sounds reasonable enough. Why would anyone take offense to that?" Aunt Fran sat back in her chair.

I could tell she had calmed down and had switched to her maternal protective mode. The very idea that someone should dare to attack one of her family members raised her hackles.

"I have a picture that I came across, don't ask me how, but I want you both to study it. I'd really like your opinion," I said as I reached into my purse and withdrew the mystery image of Hilda with the pair of soldiers. I handed the photo to my aunt first.

148

Fran stared at the picture, her brows arched, she raised wide eyes to me. "This is that dead girl. Right? Hilda? It looks like she's standing next to Bryan Kirkland, but who's the other fella?"

Fran passed the photograph over to Colleen, who also stared at the image of two men in uniform standing next to a smiling, happy Hilda Moran. She shook her head in wonder. "Which man is Bryan? I can't tell. These guys look like twins. Maybe it's the uniforms or buzz haircuts, but still. . ."

"My point exactly. I can't be sure whether Bryan is on the left or right of Hilda. Remember that telegram I showed you, Aunt Fran? This puzzle is becoming more confusing every day," I said as we each stared at the trio of smiling faces in the black and white Polaroid.

I walked through the door and confronted a welcoming committee comprising one lonely cat and one concerned but furious husband. Mittens rubbed his head against my legs, providing me some solace as I dropped my purse onto the kitchen counter and waited for Doug to begin scolding me. I began to move toward him when suddenly he engulfed me within his strong arms and crushed me to his chest. I pressed my head against his shoulder, clinging to him. We stood locked together; relief poured over me. I was home safe and sound, finally admitting to myself just how much that incident had scared me.

"Are you alright?" Doug asked as he pulled back and held me at arm's length. He studied my face with worried eyes.

"How did you know?"

"Your aunt phoned me as soon as you and Colleen left. Now tell me the entire story so I can make my own judgements."

"Not much to tell, really," I stammered, then took a deep breath. "Colleen picked me up this morning, and we went out to Oak Meadow to meet Gary Bates so we could pay the reunion's final invoice. The night of the party, I had asked Ricardo to add on the extra appetizers to our bill, but I didn't know how much that would cost. Gary agreed to wait on the final payment until the reunion committee had tallied all our tickets and expenses."

"Okay, so what happened when you got to the inn?" Doug asked. He stood with arms folded, waiting for me to continue my story.

"Colleen and I had to wait. Gary was busy in his office, so we decided to use the restroom to freshen up. That's when I thought I saw Bryan Kirkland walking down one of the corridors and I tried to follow him. Next thing I knew, someone shoved me into a broom closet and locked the door. That's all."

"Yeah, that's all, huh? Your aunt told me someone threatened you at knife point. Wanna explain that?"

"I don't know for sure if it was a knife. I never said that. I felt a cold metal pressed against my neck as I was being pushed. It might have been a knife; I don't know. I wasn't cut or anything," I said.

"That does it. I'm going out to Kirkland's place. I'm not going to stand by and have you attacked. This has gone on too far. With the evidence I saw at that motel, if he's guilty of killing that girl, then by God, I'm going to prove it and haul him in," Doug declared.

"How? Did you forget you're suspended? You know you can't use anything we found at the motel. No search warrant and illegally breaking in, how would you explain that?"

"I'll make a damn citizen's arrest if I have to. No, it's time he and I had a reckoning. I'm done pussy-footing around." Doug strode into the laundry room and unlocked his gun safe that stood against the back wall. I watched him reach for his personal Smith and Wesson, check the ammunition, and tuck the gun into his waistband.

"Why do you need the gun? What are you going to do?" I cried, seeing there was no reasoning with him.

"You don't think I'm going out there without some kind of protection? He's already killed once; he's got nothing to lose with one more dead body."

I dug my cell phone out of my purse and shoved it into my pocket then ran after my husband, slamming the back door behind me. I hurried to catch up with him and jumped into the front seat of his pickup truck.

"Where do you think you're going?" he growled.

"I'm going with you. You're in this mess because of me; if there's any danger, we'll face it together. I'm not staying home so don't try to make me," I stated and locked in my seat belt.

"When we get there, you keep out of harm's way and call 9-1-1 for help at the first sign of trouble. Promise?"

"Yes, I promise."

Chapter 18

We rode in silence as the late afternoon sun sank lower in the sky. The Kirkland Estate stretched across the hillside north of town. Ten minutes away, it seemed a short driving distance. Doug turned onto the climbing perimeter road that would lead onto the Kirkland winding driveway to arrive eventually at the mansion's front entrance. He slowed the pickup before we got too close and approached cautiously.

"Someone's here. I see a car parked near Bryan's, over there on the right, near the garages," I said as I pointed toward a black sedan.

"Might be best if we stay out of sight until I know what's going on," Doug said as he pulled the truck into a stand of trees close to the roadway and cut the engine.

We crept toward the house. Ted William's realty sign stood erected on the lawn near the entry pavers. I noticed the heavy draperies on the front windows still hung open, just as Ted had left them. We hid behind a cluster of shrubs, listening for any sounds or voices, deciding which way to move next.

"Let's go around to the left. I remember the library had a pair of French doors that opened onto a flagstone portico. Ted had unlocked them then had difficulty closing them again when we were here last. Maybe we can get into the house from there," I told Doug as we crouched low, sneaked past the wide front entrance and ran toward the corner of the house.

Shadows lengthened as daylight dimmed; faint light shown through two upper windows of the house. Downhill, at the turn of the road, a streetlamp flickered on. A stray cat streaked across my path, dashing out from under nearby bushes; it startled me, causing me to jump back so quickly that I collided with Doug and would have fallen to the ground had he not caught me. I gasped.

"Shhh, be quiet," Doug cautioned me in a whisper louder than my gasp.

"Humph," I glared at him indignantly, then pulled my hand out of his grasp. He didn't need to remind me to be quiet, I've done this before.

Creeping toward the portico, I pointed excitedly at the library door cracked open. "Look. I don't think Bryan has entered the library since Ted was here," I breathed.

The French doors opened outward from the library. One door appeared to be shut, but the left door stood slightly ajar. Doug silently stepped to the side of the door and dared a peek inside. We heard faint voices somewhere in the house. Doug strained to listen as he inched the door open, freezing when the hinges squeaked noisily. Doug waved his hand, motioning me to wait and stay hidden.

I watched as Doug slipped into the dark room. I crawled toward the open door and waited, trying to see Doug's movements while I remained out of sight. The volume of voices became louder as the hall door to the library was thrown wide; a shaft of light spilled into the shadowy room. Bryan Kirkland strode forward. I could hear someone question him, but that person remained out of sight. Where was Doug? He had to be hiding somewhere in the library.

"You have to wait. I tell you I don't have the money yet," shouted Bryan. I could just make out his movements as he stomped toward the secretary desk.

"I don't believe you," snarled a man's voice. The tone of that voice sounded familiar to me; I tried to grasp fragments of a memory buried in my mind.

"I need more time; the bank won't release the accounts until probate is complete," argued Bryan.

I heard footsteps tapping on the hardwood floor; footsteps that became muffled by the plush library carpet. I couldn't see who else had entered the library. The narrow crack of the door limited my angle of view. Frustrated, I crawled over to the other side of the French doors and tried to peer through the sheer curtains covering the glass panes. I could see legs and shoes, but little else. A tall Queen Anne chair blocked my view further into the room unless I moved, but I feared revealing my hiding place. I held my breath as one man walked near the doors. Would he notice the door ajar or assume it was only left open for air? I held my breath.

He stopped near the chair then turned and walked back toward the desk. I could just make out Bryan mumbling angrily. I peered through the crack of the door again to see Bryan pull out the narrow desk drawer and shake the contents onto the floor. His face showed his puzzlement as he fingered the pile of papers. I realized that was the drawer that had held the prom picture I took and now he must have discovered it missing.

"What's wrong?" asked the man.

"Nothing. I'm missing something, that's all. It's not important."

"You don't act like it's not important."

"Somebody has been snooping; that realtor dude was here yesterday with Meredith," Bryan said.

"That busybody; I should have done more to her than lock her in a closet," the man growled.

"You leave her alone; one dead woman is enough," Bryan snapped.

"I don't like it; her snooping is getting too close."

I gasped out loud as the memory of that voice came rushing back at me; the voice that I heard arguing with Hilda the night of her murder. That same angry growl, it had to be him. I stumbled backwards from the doorway and knocked over an empty clay pot. The crash echoed in the still night.

The occupants of the room turned as one to rush toward the open French doors. I fumbled for my phone buried in my pocket, my fingers punching buttons, groping blindly to dial 9-1-1 for help like I promised Doug, but then Bryan pushed the door wide open and quickly grabbed my arm to haul me into the room.

I kicked and twisted, trying to break his hold while I tried not to panic. I knew my husband waited close by. Wasn't he?

"Let go of me! You're hurting my arm. Let go, I say," I screamed at my captor and kicked him in his shins; I was aiming higher, but he moved, and I lost my balance.

"What are you doing here, Merry?" demanded Bryan.

Bryan hobbled to the sofa and threw me onto one end of it; he bent forward and rubbed his bruised leg, cursing me under his breath. My breath caught in my throat as I recognized Gary Bates step into the pale circle of light. Why was he here?

"You don't listen very well. I told you to back off, but here you are," sneered Gary. "Such a little busybody, can't leave well enough alone." His polished veneer of the pleasant innkeeper crumbled and revealed the crazed criminal beneath. His smile contorted into a snarl.

"You locked me in that closet," I accused, casting a frantic look about the dark room then back again to focus fully on my assailant.

"Just a tiny warning. Women don't seem to take me seriously," Gary said. He laughed and shivers went down my spine at the malicious sound.

"Bryan, what's going on here? Why is he demanding money from you?" I asked, as I glanced between the two men.

"Go ahead, *Bryan*, tell her. Tell your high school sweetheart," Gary taunted.

"Tell me what? Did you murder Hilda? Is that what this is about?"

"Shut up Merry! You don't know what you're talking about. I never killed anyone. How could I? Didn't I get stabbed? I'm the victim here," Bryan whined.

I turned to Gary and stared at him; my mind replayed the scene behind the banquet hall, hearing once again the plea from Hilda and the growling reply.

"You were the person fighting with Hilda that night. I heard her ask for her money and your voice answered her." I sought to change tactics. "Why were you paying Hilda, Gary? What was she doing for you?" I inquired. I reclined against the back of the leather sofa and tried to appear nonchalant while I prayed that he couldn't hear my heart thumping in my chest. Keep him talking, buy time, that's what Doug always advised. I just need to stay calm until help arrives or Doug makes his move.

I tried to play it smart; gain their confidence, play up to their egos and let them keep talking until they incriminated themselves. I hoped Doug could listen from wherever he was hiding. I promise, the next time he tells me to stay put and do as I'm told… I will.

Gary paced back and forth, in and out of the meager light. "Stupid broad, she traveled all the way across the country just to visit dear Bryan's home and meet his father. Too bad she got here too late; the old man had already died, but not too late to run into an old friend and realize it might be worth some cash," Gary snorted.

I studied Bryan's features, the color of his eyes, the part on his hair and suddenly that tiny nibble of memory came flooding back. When I had viewed his bare chest at the hospital, I knew something was wrong, and now I remembered what.

"Who are you? I know you're not Bryan Kirkland. Bryan had a strawberry birthmark on his left shoulder, just below the collarbone.

158

You don't have a mark like that. So, who are you and what happened to the real Bryan?" I demanded, as I confronted the man sitting next to me. How could I not have seen the difference?

Bryan laughed, a dismissive sound, and threw up his hands. "Well Gary, looks like your goose with the golden egg just laid a dud. The jig's up."

He turned to me, extended his hand, as he answered, "My name's Greg Ginder, from Tuscaloosa, Alabama. Nice to meet you, máam." He chuckled again, then dropped his hand when I failed to shake it. "Bryan and I met at boot camp and then ran across each other again out in Fort Irwin when we deployed to Iraq. We used to joke and say we were brothers from another mother because the resemblance was so strong. Hell, we used to play tricks on the Army when one of us had a weekend pass and the other would use it. No one could tell us apart, except Hilda. She and Bryan had a thing."

The two men in Hilda's photograph. . . now it made sense. "Why was Hilda killed; because she knew you?"

"Gary overheard me and Hilda talking one day at that diner she worked in. Just my luck old Gary here chose that one day to stop for coffee on his drive back from Columbus. Hilda threatened to go to the cops and turn me in for fraud, but I begged her to wait and promised her I'd do right by Buddy's memory."

"Buddy, you mean Bryan?"

"Yeah, that was Hilda's nickname for him."

"Okay, but I heard Hilda demanding her money. Who was supposed to pay her, you or Gary?" I asked.

159

"I was paying Gary, not Hilda. He cornered me one night at the Inn and offered to stay quiet for a reasonable sum of money; his idea of reasonable and mine differ greatly, the bloodsucker. Oh yeah, he told me he knew all about my little scam and would turn me into the cops if I didn't pay up," Greg/Bryan grumbled.

"Hilda and me, we had a deal; she was supposed to provide me with hard evidence of Bryan's death and Greg's impersonation. I needed more than hearsay to hold over his head, to really cash in. I promised to pay her a thousand dollars for the information. Seemed like a pretty good bargain to me but she got greedy and demanded more," Gary said with a snicker. His right hand slowly reached behind his back and pulled a revolver from his waistband. He waved the gun menacingly toward me and Greg/Bryan, then motioned us to stand and walk toward the hallway.

"You didn't need to kill Hilda, Gary. She was a sweet gal. I tried to stop him, Merry, honest. That's when he stabbed me, just to drive home his point, he said. I got the message all right," Greg/Bryan whined.

"How did Bryan die? I saw the letter from the Army," I said. I dragged my feet, deliberately delaying our departure hoping Doug would have a chance to act.

"We were on a patrol in Iraq; our Humvee hit an IED. I got injured but Buddy took the hit and was killed instantly, blown to pieces. I knew the stockade waited for me because of some black-market deals I had going, so I swapped dog tags with Bryan and hoped we could switch identities one last time. It worked too, for a while," Greg explained.

"I don't understand. What could you hope to gain? The Army would eventually identify the body with all their tests; you had to know that."

"Yeah, well, I was hoping to cash in on Bryan's trust account and disappear with the money until Gary here threw a monkey wrench into my plans."

"Why didn't you tell the police that Gary stabbed you? You could have identified him as the murderer," I said.

"How could I? If I had accused him, he would've turned me in for fraud – identity theft and embezzlement. I'm between a rock and a hard place," Greg/Bryan moaned.

"Enough gab, you two. I'm tired of hearing your life stories. You," Gary yelled and pointed to Greg/Bryan, "make out that check and sign it. Make sure you add at least six zeros on the end of that number. Then you two are going to have a terrible accident and I'm going on a long vacation," Gary chortled, pleased with his own wit.

I spotted a dark shape across the room as Doug crawled out from where he had crouched behind a massive sideboard. He kept to the deep corners of the room as he silently crept toward Gary Bates. I cast a glance to watch my husband and turned to stare once more at the gun pointed menacingly at me and Greg.

Suddenly, I spied Doug prepare to leap out of the dark shadows behind Gary as we inched toward the hallway. Our eyes locked. I had to think quickly. What would Doug want me to do? I pretended to

161

faint and latched onto Greg/Bryan's arm, pulling him down with me as I collapsed onto the floor.

Doug shouted, "Hold it Bates. Drop that gun. You're under arrest." He rushed forward, pointing his own gun on the suspect at the split second that I dropped to the ground.

Gary Bates spun around and tried to run for the open French door. Doug leaped to tackle him. Bates fired one wild round before Doug kicked the gun away from his hand. I screamed as Greg/Bryan shoved me in a rolling motion into the hallway, away from the line of fire. I could hear his own grunt of pain while Doug pinned Bates to the floor.

"Not again," moaned Greg/Bryan as he clutched his shoulder, red blood seeped through his fingers and ran down the front of his shirt. "I didn't get injured this much in Iraq."

"He's been shot," I cried, as I crawled back to him and pressed his torn shirt against the wound.

"Call for help," Doug directed me as he grabbed a curtain tieback to use as makeshift handcuffs on Bates. He tied the cord tightly around the man's wrists then forced him into one of the library chairs while we waited for backup.

My fingers shook as I dialed the number and gave our address to the operator. Within minutes the night sky filled with red flashing strobes and sirens shrilled as multiple police and emergency vehicles crowded onto the Kirkland property.

Sheriff Edgar Simmons was the first to enter the house and survey the scene. He saw me crouched on the floor with Greg and Doug standing guard next to a subdued Gary Bates.

"Huh, Sargent Gardner, I see you have matters well in hand and can present a full explanation of the events here. I'll expect that report on my desk first thing in the morning. By the way, Doug, you seemed to have left a few things behind at the station," Simmons stated as he tossed Doug's badge to him. "Nobody suspends my officers but me."

"Yes sir, I can. Thank you, sir."

Simmons turned to his deputies and the paramedics, then pointed to Greg and commanded, "Get this man to the hospital. And Dalton, be sure he doesn't go anywhere after they patch him up."

The young rookie deputy saluted and climbed into the ambulance to accompany Greg Ginder back to the hospital.

Chapter 19

Voices buzzed around my crowded dining table. Mugs of coffee and hot tea, along with slices of warm cinnamon streusel cake, were served as everyone spoke at once, eager for details and answers. Aunt Fran hovered over me protectively, smiling and hugging me every few minutes. Colleen breathed a sigh of relief that our confrontation with Gary Bates at Oak Meadows had been limited.

Martha Parker and Barbara Williams joked with Anna Thompson about the strangest class reunion the town ever experienced.

I sipped my coffee and gazed upon this collection of friends and family who had rushed to my support and who had helped solve the murder of a poor, innocent woman. A sense of deep gratitude and love swept over me. I felt so lucky and blessed to be surrounded by a wonderful, caring group of people.

I knuckle-rubbed Mittens on the top of his head as he purred his approval. He curled up on my lap, content to linger and receive my attention.

"How did you know Gary was guilty?" asked Aunt Fran.

"I didn't. Believe me, no one was more surprised than me when he walked into that library. Heck, I always thought he was such a polite, gentle man, but it was all an act," I said as I stuck my fork into a piece of cake. "Mmm, Martha this streusel is delicious. Thank you so much for treating us."

"I'm just happy to know you're safe and that horrible murderer is behind bars," Martha replied. A murmur of voices rose in agreement.

"You know, if we ladies hadn't learned Hilda's identity, her death might have gone unsolved. Our sleuthing skills proved valuable once again. I think we all deserve a pat on the back," drawled Anna.

"It's so hard to believe that poor Bryan died over in Iraq and never had a proper funeral. His poor father, what he must have gone through. I really thought Greg was Bryan; they could be twins," Colleen said.

"At least Doug is cleared and back on duty. I hear Simmons gave those state troopers the heave ho," Aunt Fran chuckled. "And weren't you the clever one to record the entire conversation and confessions on your phone!"

"Um, well, that was really an accident. I had tried to press 9-1-1 before I was caught by Greg, but since I couldn't see what I was doing, I mistakenly pressed the record feature on my camera. Turned out okay in the end and I did phone for help eventually," I admitted with a sheepish grin.

"What was Greg going to do with that prom picture? I don't understand why he took that," Colleen commented.

"Guess he was afraid someone would study it too closely and make the comparison between him and the photo and realize there was a difference," I said.

We shared our memories of a former classmate while I attempted to answer everyone's worries and reach a state of peace in my own mind. I reached for the coffee pot and freshened cups around the table. The coffee cake had dwindled to a remaining slice or two.

"I'll always remember Bryan for the funny stunts he did in school, such a clown. He loved practical jokes. How about that time we were all down at the lake and he swung out on that frayed rope and the thing broke? He fell head-first into the middle of that lake; I swear we all feared he drowned until he popped up next to us on the shore," Martha recalled. "Scared the daylights out of me."

"Mm-hmm, I kept seeing him in my mind's eye, remembering all the swim parties we had and that birthmark of his. Finally, that strawberry mark registered in my brain, and I realized that was what was different about Greg and Bryan. When I saw him in the hospital with his shirt off, I kept staring at his chest thinking something was wrong, but I just couldn't put my finger on it. I might never have guessed he wasn't Bryan, if he hadn't been hurt,"

"How did this Greg know so much information about you and Meadowood or was all that just an act too?" asked Aunt Fran.

"He admitted to me that Bryan used to talk about me and his hometown when he and Greg were in boot camp. Guess Bryan was a bit homesick and shared pictures and stories with him. Greg gave himself away, though, when he started criticizing OSU and the Buckeyes; Bryan would never have done that. His masquerade couldn't have lasted," I explained to the group.

A rapid tapping on the back door drew my attention and I called out to the visitor, "Come on in, door's open!"

Ted Williams rushed into the room and glanced around at the gathering of women. His flushed face mirrored his anxiety as he declined a place to sit and preferred to pace the floor space between the dining and living room.

"Is it true? Bryan Kirkland is actually dead; this fella was only impersonating him?" Ted questioned.

"Afraid so. Looks like your listing is null and void. Greg Ginder pretended to be Bryan Kirkland to swindle the estate, pure and simple," I said. Poor Ted: that real estate sale meant so much to him, the highlight of his career.

Barb jumped up from her seat and wrapped an arm about her husband's shoulder. "It's okay, Honey. There'll be other listings."

A glimmer of hope leapt into his eyes, "What happens to the house now? Maybe I can still sell it for the new owner."

"Sorry. From what Doug learned, Earl Kirkland's last will and testament deeded the house and lands to Bryan then in the event of his death, the entire property is to be donated to the county with the provisions that the home be converted into a half-way house and shelter for homeless veterans. Really a good cause, don't you think?" I stated.

The sun shone brightly in a cloudless sky that couldn't get any bluer as Doug and I drove our minivan northward on Friday morning to retrieve our two sons. They'd had a longer than planned visit with Doug's parents, and now I was eager to get them home again. The quiet in the house needed some disruption, as only two young boys could provide. Even Mittens missed the boys chasing after him.

We drove past multiple Amish communities and miles of rich farmlands, then skirted past the Cleveland metropolitan area as we neared Shaker Heights on the Lake. To my delight, Billy and Johnny waited on the front porch and waved wildly as we pulled into the drive. I leapt from the van before the engine stopped and gathered both of my boys into a fierce hug.

"I missed you both very much," I cried. I smothered them in kisses as they squirmed to break away.

"Aww Mom. You're squishing me," complained Billy.

"What 'cha been doing while we've been here?" asked Johnny.

Doug and I exchanged glances as we both answered, "Not much." We laughed and hugged our boys again. Our lives were never dull.

SCARECROWS and CORPSES

A Meadowood Mystery - Book 1

Meredith Gardner is a busy wife, mother and homemaker who volunteers her time on food drives, as Scout den mother, Avon saleswoman and as a classroom assistant at the local elementary school. She's got a curious mind and instinct for what's happening in her beloved community.

What will happen when Merry (Meredith), and her scout troop find a body in a local Halloween corn maze? Who did the dastardly deed? Someone in town is not whom they pretend to be. When a friend is accused of murder, Merry is determined to prove him innocent and find the true killer. Murder and mayhem confront Merry as she protects her own son's life and outwits a diabolical killer on the spookiest night of the year.

Follow Meredith along with her pet cat, Mittens, as she enlists her friends to help solve this cozy mystery amongst the Halloween ghouls and goblins roaming about their rural, mid-western town of Meadowood.

Author Biography

A resident of central Ohio for over 40 years; Nancy M. Wade and her husband Gary now claim the hills of Tennessee as home.

Her works combine romance and mystery with warm characters set in historic timeframes and locales or cozy, homey settings.

Nancy M. Wade's novels include the romantic suspense Circle-D Sagas: *Endless Circle* and *Moment in Time;* a rich family drama, *Reflections: A Sentimental Journey;* a historical romance novel, *Frontier Heart;* plus, a contemporary short story called *Courtship of Laura.* Her latest work is the cozy mystery series titled *A Meadowood Mystery* with the first book in that series *Scarecrows and Corpses.* All of her books are available for order online in both paperback or E-book formats on Amazon.com, Barnes & Noble, Books-a-Million and Indie Bound.

A Note from the Author:

I hope you enjoyed reading **Reunion with Death.** If you would like to leave a review, please go to www.amazon.com or www.goodreads.com and do so today. I love hearing what readers have to say about my stories and characters.

Connect with me on social media with my Facebook page: https://www.facebook.com/authorNancyMWade/

You can also follow my blog on my web site: https://nancymwade.com and send me a message if you would like to request a signed, personalized copy of my book.

Thank you! Nancy

Made in the USA
Monee, IL
11 May 2024

58340889R00098